THE GALILEAN JEWISHNESS OF JESUS

Studies in Judaism and Christianity

Exploration of Issues in the Contemporary Dialogue Between Christians and Jews

Editor in Chief for
Stimulus Books
Helga Croner

Editors
Lawrence Boadt, C.S.P.
Helga Croner
Leon Klenicki
John Koenig
Kevin A. Lynch, C.S.P.

 A STIMULUS BOOK

CONVERSATION ON THE ROAD NOT TAKEN
Volume One

THE GALILEAN JEWISHNESS OF JESUS

Retrieving the Jewish Origins of Christianity

Bernard J. Lee, S.M.

A STIMULUS BOOK

PAULIST PRESS ♦ NEW YORK ♦ MAHWAH

Artwork by Steve Erspamer.

Excerpts from the essays of Henry Slonimsky are reprinted by permission of Hebrew Union College Press, Cincinnati, Ohio.

Library of Congress Cataloging-in-Publication Data

Lee, Bernard J., 1932-
    The Galilean Jewishness of Jesus.

    (Studies in Judaism and Christianity) (A
Stimulus book)
        Bibliography: p.
        1. Jesus Christ—Knowledge—Judaism.   2. Jesus
Christ—Knowledge—Civilization, Greco-Roman.
3. Judaism—History—Post-exilic period,
586 B.C.-210 A.D.   4. Civilization, Greco-Roman.
5. Christianity—Origin   6. Christianity—
Philosophy.   7. Jesus Christ—Person and
offices.   8. Jesus Christ—History of doc-
trines—Early church, ca. 30-600.
9. Bible. N.T.—Criticism, interpretation,
etc.   I.Title.   II. Series.
BT590.J8L43 1988   232.9'03   88-22515
ISBN 0-8091-3021-1 (pbk.)

Published by Paulist Press
997 Macarthur Boulevard
Mahwah, N.J. 07430

Printed and bound in the
United States of America

Contents

PREFACE

I shall be telling this with a sigh
Somewhere ages and ages hence:
Two roads diverged in a wood, and I—
I took the one less travelled by.
And that has made all the difference.

Robert Frost

There are so many lives I might have lived besides the one I concretely live at this moment. Whether I have affection for or resentment toward this present life's configuration, I must acknowledge that it could have been so other. It still could be so other. Something else might be the case. This is what the Czech novelist Milan Kundera calls "the unbearable lightness of being."[1] We like to impose the heaviness of an inexorable logic or an absolutely detailed providence upon the actual stories our lives tell. With that fiction of "heaviness" our present stories, for better and for worse, seem easier to embrace. But closer to the truth are the million "might have beens" that insist upon the fragility of any actual world. Free choices and inscrutable chances collude with an elusive providence to make us what we are today. But *it* could have been otherwise, *I* could have been otherwise, *we* could have been otherwise—and perhaps with no less integrity!

Most of us, most of the time, instinctively take the roads with the most human traffic. We are socialized to do so. Sometimes we do it simply because we'd rather not walk so alone. But in our unguarded moments we wonder what it might be like right now had we taken the less travelled road. Sometimes our imaginings are quiet and peaceful, other times provocative, and sometimes downright fierce. They are fiercest when the present is full of suffering and the alternative coaxes us with splendid (even if dubious) promise. The popularity of Frost's poem, "The Road Not Taken," has much to do with how well his words name the poignancy and the ache of our "might have beens."

For me, much of the power of Frost's poem lies in the final line: "And that has made all the difference." There is always some fascination in entertaining all those "might have beens." But only when I *seriously explore the roads I didn't take* do I begin to understand what difference it makes that I *happen* to be here where I am now. This serious exploration often opens me to a legitimate "something else that might be the case," and then I stand before marvelous possibility. Time becomes fecund. In such a moment I am suddenly

1

alert again to the "lightness" of my present place in life. In this moment I also feel my openness to the many roads that suddenly appear before me—an intuition into what the philosophers and theologians call self-transcendence, and sometimes simply name as freedom.

Freedom is not always pleasant. It was people who ached with freedom that Dostoevsky names in "The Legend of the Grand Inquisitor" in his novel *The Brothers Karamazov*. To bear the full responsibility of choosing one's own road from among all the possible roads can be so painful that people lay their freedom before the Church and ask: "Will *you* please give me the logic of my life that I might follow it?" The "lightness" of being is found unbearable. In our own century Jean-Paul Sartre says that "condemned to freedom" is the existential character of human existence.

For reasons that I hope will be clear in the three volumes that follow, retrieving the Jewishness of Jesus means refinding what was a less travelled road in the very early years of Christian life. That less travelled road became a virtually abandoned road. Because of the undergrowth and overgrowth, the more Jewish road has not even been noted on our doctrinal maps.

Above all, I care about sensing all the difference the less travelled road might have made. It is time to reopen that road once again to normal Christian traffic.

I know how commonplace it is for a theologian to say "this book is an experiment" or "my proposals are but an initial foray into the territory being explored." Commonplace or not, I feel that deeply. But my own interest in this topic has alerted me to some of the "lightness" of Christian being. Or, to say the same thing differently, my walks on the less travelled road give me a sense of the manifold something elses that might be the case.

Monika Hellwig has recently described one of the roles of the theologian as that of the archaeologist, "one who makes new discoveries that may well upset old theories and old justifications for present practices."[2] Archaeological findings often relativize the interpretations of history with which we have long lived. Uncovering the Jewishness of Jesus, a case in point, relativizes all the supersessionist christologies that are signposts along most Christian highways. For me, the discovery reinforces what I find increasingly to be the incredible suppleness of the Good News of Jesus Christ.

Hellwig rightly notes that for a Catholic, fidelity to truth must be wed to fidelity to community solidarity. "The discoveries of the past, and the discoveries of the natural and human sciences, cannot in conscience be falsified, but we can endeavor to set them in the context of the whole mystery of redemption, of the acknowledgement of sin, but also of grace.''[3] In service to the community of faith, Hellwig says that theology must always open itself to dialogue and challenge. It is for that reason that I want to affirm over and over the character of the three volumes that follow as open and ongoing conversation.

People like Karl Rahner[4] and Walbert Buhlmann[5] have been alerting Roman Catholics to the implications of becoming a world church after nearly nineteen hundred years as a largely European phenomenon. (The cultural ties between the U.S. church and the European church are huge.) What might it be like to let the Good News loose? Really to let it grow up in vastly different cultural appropriations? In his novel *Silence,* Shusaku Endo has posed the question with immense drama. A Catholic priest missionary, in order to remain in Japan where he can then continue to be interactive with Japanese, must trample underfoot a bronze image of Christ crucified that he brought with him from his European country. It is a precious image that stands for the commitments of his whole life. This image, attached to a board, is called a *fumie.* If he is to remain a living presence among the people of Japan, he must surrender his own cultural Christ by trampling publicly on the *fumie.* How much, really, can we separate Christ from our conditioned images of him? There is no culturally unconditioned Christ. The missionary speaks:

'Lord, since long, long ago, innumerable times have I thought of your face. Especially since coming to this country I have done so tens of times. . . . Whenever I prayed your face appeared before me; when I was alone I thought of your face imparting a blessing; when I was captured your face as it appeared when you carried your cross gave me life. This face is deeply ingrained in my soul—the most beautiful, the most precious thing in the world has been living in my heart. And now with this foot I am going to trample it.'

The first rays of the dawn appear. The light shines on his long neck stretched out like a chicken and upon the bony shoulders. The priest grasps the *fumie* with both hands bringing it close to his eyes. He would like to press to his own face that face trampled on by so many feet. With saddened glance he stares intently at the man in the center of the *fumie,* worn down and hollow from the constant trampling [from others]. A tear is about to fall from his eye. 'Ah,' he says trembling, 'the pain!'

'It is only a formality. What do formalities matter?' The interpreter urges him on excitedly. 'Only go through the exterior form of trampling.'

The priest raises his foot. In it he feels a dull, heavy pain. This is no mere formality. He will not trample on what he has considered the most beautiful thing in his life, on what he has believed most pure, on what is filled with the ideals and the dreams of man. How his foot aches! And the Christ in bronze speaks to the priest: 'Trample! Trample! I more than anyone else know of the pain in your foot. Trample! It was to be trampled on by men that I was born into this world. It was to share man's pain that I carried my cross.'

The priest placed his foot on the *fumie*. Dawn broke. And far in the distance the cock crew.[6]

Endo's narrative signals immense ambiguity. How risky is it to let the fully familiar christological grasp of Jesus go in order that he might reappear in dress we may not recognize? At stake is the very thing we have found most pure, the most beautiful thing in our lives, the source of our dreams and ideals. If we allow the christological meaning of Jesus to develop down another road than the Graeco-Roman road it actually took, is it truth or treason? Does the Christ-event itself require the development? Is it the *fumie* speaking? Or is the thrice crowing cock telling the truth?

While I am also deeply interested in what an indigenous Japanese or Indian appropriation of Jesus might be, I am convinced that the Jewish option is perhaps the most important test case. I am not, of course, talking about Jews appropriating Jesus. I mean the Christian retrieval of Jesus' Jewishness. That's the "something else that might be the case" in which I am interested. Jesus was after all precisely the Jew whose Jewishness the mainstream Christian tradition has at least suppressed and at worst hated.

All I can say at this moment is that I have begun to walk down the less travelled road and for me it has made all the difference. And I am eager to share a preliminary report with anyone who will join me in the conversation. Who knows what we shall perhaps "be telling with a sigh / Somewhere ages and ages hence"?

Bernard J. Lee, S.M.
San Antonio, July 1988

Notes

1. Milan Kundera, *The Unbearable Lightness of Being* (New York: Harper, 1984), pp. 3–6.

2. Monika Hellwig, *The Role of the Theologian* (Kansas City: Sheed & Ward, 1987), pp. 39–40.

3. Hellwig, 1987, pp. 40–41.

4. Karl Rahner, "Towards a Fundamental Theological Interpretation of Vatican II," *Theological Studies* 40 (1979), pp. 716–727

5. Walbert Buhlman, *The Coming of the Third Church* (Maryknoll: Orbis, 1977).

6. Shusaku Endo, *Silence* (New York: Taplinger, 1976), pp. 258–259.

INTRODUCTION

> The struggle between Athens and Jerusalem indeed has taken many forms: it is the conflict between philosophy and the church, Greek wisdom and Jewish Torah, reason and faith, the secular and the sacred—or, in another transformation, Christian and Jew. It has involved the best minds of the West and spilled over into every epoch, taking another guise, using another language but continuing old quarrels and flirtations.
>
> *The Slayers of Moses*
> Susan A. Handelman[1]

Within decades after the death of Jesus, Greek Jewish Christians are reproaching the Hebrew Jewish Christians in Jerusalem because the latter are taking better care of their own widows (Acts 6:1–6). A century and a half later Tertullian ponders whether the distance between Christians and Jews is parallel to that between Athens and Jerusalem. He may be the first to give the question that explicit formulation, but the so-called Council of Jerusalem (c. 58–59 CE) has already suffered the anguish of the issue.

Paul and Barnabas are leaders of the Antioch community when delegates from Jerusalem arrive to reprove them for not requiring pagans who follow Jesus to be circumcised (Acts 15:1–35). After a long argument with them, Paul and Barnabas decide to go to Jerusalem themselves to deal with the Jerusalem community and its leaders, principal among them being James, the brother of the Lord. Pharisees who are believers in Jesus are lodging protests; they want circumcision and compliance with the Law of Moses from non-Jews who choose to follow Jesus.

Paul and Barnabas meet with the apostles (Peter among them), the elders and the assembled community. Peter reasons that since the Spirit enables pagans to believe in Jesus, no unnecessary burdens should be laid upon them, especially those which Jews themselves find insupportable. Then, speaking from Isaiah, James recalls that a restored House of Israel is destined to offer God's salvation to all people. At this time the being of the church is still understood to belong to the being of Israel. James listens, and then rules (he is clearly the church leader at this point) that four prescriptions must be maintained: abstaining from anything polluted by idols, from fornication, from the meat of strangled animals, and from blood. It is a compromise. James has maintained at least some minimal behavioral connections with Judaism. Paul and Barnabas feel vindicated that circumcision and the whole Torah are not imposed. Along with representatives from the Jerusalem community, they take the happy news back to Antioch.

Luke's sanguine account, however, misses the fierceness that Paul owns in his letter to the Galatians. He accuses the Jerusalem people of spying on Antioch, and says he told Peter that he, Peter, was wrong and was behaving like a pagan. What happened between Paul and Peter is not precisely clear from either account, but there's nothing unclear about Paul's anger.

The Jerusalem decision favored the growing group of Hellenized converts to Jesus. However, we must not miss the point that this was a local conflict, and the solution proposed was for the communities of Syria and Cilicia. Neither Antioch nor Jerusalem could have foreseen the hugely Greek shape of church that evolved, nor the effects of that Jerusalem decision when applied to other situations for which it was not originally intended.

Like many Christians, I used to applaud the Jerusalem church for freeing up the Christian story—and I still do applaud the decision as a local solution for a local problem. But as I have recognized more and more fully the utter Jewishness of Jesus, I judge that the decision, when generalized beyond its local circumstances, has driven a wedge between Christian faith and the Jewish faith that was, and could still be in many ways, its nurturing matrix.

I shall be saying in all that follows that I believe the distance between Athens and Jerusalem is roughly parallel to the distance between Western Christians and Jews. I am not the first to say this, but I hope that I shall be saying it for new reasons, and can perhaps point to some ways to engage Jewish roots more fully in Christian self-understanding. I especially want to avoid the position that the differences are ''merely'' cultural or ''merely'' linguistic.

Historical consciousness is a constant reminder that there is no such thing as one single human culture, there are only multiple human cultures. We are not born into a genetically defined human world in the way that members of the animal kingdom are born into their respective animal worlds. It is human nature that we make our human world, that is, we make culture which reciprocally makes us. The culture we make is the story out of which we live. It is our deep story. There are multiple deep stories which human beings have made. It is my conviction that profound contrasts exist between the world of Galilean Jews in Jesus' time and the Greek world that became the nurturing matrix for the emergence of a Christian church and a profound tradition of Christian doctrine.

The benefit of our age is that we can better recognize some of the serious contrasts between the root metaphors of Judaism and Hellenism. Root metaphors are not decorative elaborations of a culture, they are fonts. The cognitive structures, the formative emotions, and the religious intuitions that proceed organically from a root metaphor belong to a system, so that even where cultures have shared material, the interpretive systems that envelop the shared world are not identical.

I want to be clear about the limitations of this work. I am not suggesting that reflection upon the meaning of Jesus that does not transgress his Galilean world should be substituted for later developments. That would be silly, and the first silliness would be over-confidence that we understand Jesus' Galilean world sufficiently well to attempt it. It would be equally silly to ignore the retrieval of that Jewish world which contemporary historical, hermeneutical, and archeological studies have facilitated.

If my intention is not to substitute a Galilean interpretation of Jesus for a Greek interpretation of Jesus, for the same reason it is crucial that neither of these hold new cultural appropriations in bondage because neither of those cultural worlds of meaning is our assumptive world today.

I do not therefore want to suggest a substitute christology. Rather, I want to introduce into the christological conversation a new participant, one which earlier history excluded, when the less travelled road of Galilean Jewish interpretation was closed off for further travel. I would wish that another local decision had been made somewhere else in the first century that would have held on to more Judaism than James finally retained, so that the Jewish voice of Jesus would have had a benevolent environing matrix to help later ages hear it better on its own ground. I would wish that Ebionite instincts would have been brought into a fuller conversation rather than excluded and forced into non-dialogic isolation. I would wish that early Syrian and Armenian communities had been retained as fuller spokespersons in the creation of Christian self-understanding. We might have had a Spirit christology as compelling as our Logos christology, and concomitantly, a humanity of Jesus as accessible as the divinity of Jesus.

In fact, I wish that I knew more right now about the life of those early eastern Christian communities as well as about some of their contemporary expressions. But that is a future project. I feel I have waited long already as this project grew and grew; for as it did, I experienced more and more exasperation about the uncontainable boundaries of the discussion. So I have chosen to have a first say now, and will perhaps say more later.

I do not doubt that many of my Jewish brothers and sisters will find my proposals insufficient. Many of my Christian sisters and brothers will find them over-sufficient in their Jewishness, but insufficient for carrying the weight of two thousand years of accumulated Christian experience. To the latter I want to reiterate the limitation of the project: not to say everything, only to say something true that deserves to be a fuller participant in the social reconstruction of Christian reality at the end of the second millennium, and most especially at the end of that century which henceforth and forever must remember the Holocaust. Since the Holocaust, the retrieval of Jesus' Jewishness must belong at the heart of Christianity's social reconstruction.

To say that the church is *semper reformanda* is to recognize that creative transformation (another way of saying social reconstruction) belongs to the nature of ecclesial existence. "Re-forming" doesn't have the necessary connotation of popular usage that suggests correcting abuses, although that is sometimes included. More importantly, reformation is also a response to the symbiotic relationship between faith and culture, and the need therefore (as the Pharisees knew so well) to reinterpret our religious life on-goingly in conversation with our culture. The post-Holocaust relationship between Christianity and Judaism is immensely significant not just for those two participants but for its importance in world culture and in the future of Israel.

I hope I may conclude this introduction with some autobiographical tracings about my interest in the Jewishness of Jesus, because I think this illuminates the project I have undertaken. The tracings are both religious and philosophical.

My undergraduate philosophy degree focused almost entirely upon scholastic (esp. neo-Thomist) philosophy. Graduate work in Latin and Greek increased my fascination with Greek thought. Then during a five year period of high school teaching in St. Louis, I began reading Gabriel Marcel whose name kept turning up in conversations and in reading. While Greek philosophy (especially Aristotle) had easily engaged my mind, Marcel's work hooked me in deeply feeling ways, as well as providing intellectual challenge. I most appreciated his reminder that experience itself is not perfectly orderly and angular, but often random and meandering. He would so often walk me through experience and only afterward engage in more abstract reflection, but aware of its limitations and ready always to walk directly back into messy experience. I appreciated his appreciation for novels and theater as a mode of philosophical reflection. I took all the orderly outlines that I had prepared for my high school religion classes and burned them, and resolved to let each class evolve anew ever after. I had originally thought my outlines would have perennial value and usage!

The next significant encounter was with the then suspect work of Pierre Teilhard de Chardin. I had never heard of process philosophy at that time; but without my knowing it Teilhard was my entry into that world. Teilhard brought with him Henri Bergson and Maurice Blondel. I was delighted when I learned later that when Blondel directed attention to social action (when his writings were coming under fire), he held meetings in a Marianist institution in Paris (the basement of the Collège Stanislaus).

I understand better in retrospect that what attracted me to Teilhard was his desire to replace a two-world view with a one-world view, and to see God and world as *naturally* open to each other in mutual experience. I began to understand how Pelagianism was a fault within one system and a vital insight within another (Teilhard was aware that his work would inspire accusations of Pelagianism). Pelagianism is a heresy that presupposes a two-world view, and disallows traffic between natural and supernatural without the intervention of grace from the supernatural side.

The payoff for me in Teilhard's work was the spirituality that issued from his approach. *The Divine Milieu* assured me of the holiness of the world, the holiness of matter, and the availability of the living God in my direct experience of the world. I think it is perhaps a gift from my family that I want to take the world seriously and that I want my affection for the world to be tinged with ultimacy. I have never wanted to ignore the world to be with God. My family gave me ground-loving feet. And Teilhard gave me a ground-loving God.

When I began seminary study at the age of thirty-one I was not in the least prepared for the pain that would ensue. Our theological formation at the University of Fribourg was concentrated upon a daily course in moral theology and another in dogma. We used only the *Summa* of St. Thomas, and our lectures were in Latin. In four years no one ever asked a question in class. I am deeply grateful for those concentrated years of study of the *Summa*. It is not possible to be a Catholic theologian without being thoroughly conversant with that tradition. I found it lovely and strong. But after the journey I had already begun, I knew this world could no longer be my instinctive home.

I began to read Rudolf Bultmann on my own, and that is where my religious world began to collapse. I did not confront the project of demythologization with anyone with whom I might be in conversation. Notwithstanding an opening on the part of Pius XII, historical biblical criticism had made no significant inroads into Catholic scripture studies. At first encounter, historical consciousness takes on classical consciousness with a vengeance.

As religious meaning collapsed around me, I had recourse more and more to philosophy. I registered in the philosophy department and completed a licentiate in contemporary philosophy at the same time as the final two years of theology. During this time I read Martin Heidegger since Bultmann's indebtedness to him was so strong. I immediately appreciated his commitment to beginning the discussion of Being with an analysis of the being that was most available: our own being-in-the-world.

Then there was a happy accident. I registered for what I thought was to be a course in Kant, but turned out to be a course in the philosophy of Alfred North Whitehead with Professor I. Bochenski. The entire philosophical system felt like home. After the collapse of so many of my own religious moorings, Whitehead's natural theology seduced both mind and heart. I wrote a licentiate thesis on Whitehead's natural theology, and soon after I encountered the work of John B. Cobb, Jr. and Norman Pittenger, little dreaming that both of them would later be respected personal friends and colleagues. These two were my first theological mentors in process theology.

Whitehead once remarked that, as far as religion goes, Catholics do most of the right things, but for most of the wrong reasons. That may be an over-statement, but it has some truth. As I began to rebuild some faith structures with the help of process theology, I found myself doing nearly everything I was always doing, but for a lot of new and different reasons.

I cannot overstate my indebtedness to process theism for making to me the gift of what Christians have long called the "Old" Testament. I have since come to prefer Earlier and Later Scriptures to Old and New Testament, because these alternative expressions are not so loaded with supersessionist ideologies (that in Christ the Old Testament is abrogated and then transcended). Since Vatican II, in *Nostra Aetate,* affirms that God's covenant with the Jews continues unabated, the custom of calling that covenant "Old" in the sense of "surpassed" must itself be surpassed. If process modes of thought gave me the Jewish Scriptures, it is these same Earlier Scriptures that in their turn gave the Later Scriptures of my own Christian tradition back to me with a kind of integrity I had not experienced before.

My earliest fascination with process modes of thought was with White-head's philosophical categories and the intricacies of his immense rational system. I was reading Whitehead along with the work of Charles Hartshorne. During my doctoral work at the Graduate Theological Union I began serious historical critical scripture studies and was reading George Herbert Mead, William James and John Dewey at the same time as Whitehead. Under Bernard Loomer's tutelage I began to understand the genius of Whitehead's philosophical empiricism, and to see the fertility of religious empiricism. Because of its long commitment to a rational tradition, it has not always been easy in Catholic theology to insist upon an experiential basis for *all* theological reflection. The mood, however, has changed even in the last two decades. Bernard Lonergan's empirical concerns in theological method have been well taken (though they differ from American empiricism).

My first connection with the rational system of process metaphysics and process theism endeared me to the Hebrew concept of God. The second connection into the process world was an empirical-historical one. And this deepened my appreciation for the experiential ways that Hebrews had of naming God: God-names regularly contained allusions to the events in which God was experienced: the God who led us out of Egypt; the Father of Abraham, Isaac and Jacob; the God who made Covenant with us through Moses, etc. Along with recognizing the historically conditioned nature of all inter-pretations of God came the gradual recognition (I shamefacedly acknowledge how long it took!) that process modes of thought are one interpretation among many. And with that, the pressure I felt to be critical of Thomism abated. Today I am not entirely comfortable with process theism either. No system fully explores the mystery of a single atom, much less the far reaches of deity.

I have paid increasing attention to Whitehead's own insistence that all of his philosophical categories are tentative, are subject to further challenge from lived experience, will someday be transcended, and are in fact metaphors for experience, metaphors that cry out for an imaginative leap on our part. With this awareness came a headlong plunge into hermeneutical philosophy, particularly that of Paul Ricoeur and Hans-Georg Gadamer. I am indebted to David Tracy's work for his rich understanding of the analogical character of human thought, i.e., the nature of the analogical imagination, and for his careful analysis of interpretation in the maintenance of our classic texts.

It was also about this time that I began to understand the Pharisees as "interpreters" par excellence who opened Judaism to the future. They did not use the interpretive language of our age, of course, but they were doing it. They had to deal with the common human propensity to canonize their own interpretations, especially as the Oral Torah was committed to writing in the Mishnah. Yet the Mishnah was no sooner redacted than the tradition was expanded to contain an authoritative supplement (the Tosefta). The Mishnah then aquired profound elaboration in two versions of the Talmud. These texts are often in the form of dialogue between contrasting interpretations.

In their more faithful moments, the Pharisees and Rabbis did not so much canonize a particular interpretation as they did canonize the process of interpreting. That does not mean that they lacked moral assurance about their interpretations. One would not accuse the Rabbis of being wishy-washy! They understood their interpreting to be God's work among them, and they accorded it a normative place in their religious lives. For me, grappling with the contemporary hermeneutical tradition was also an exercise in the hermeneutics of retrieval—recovering some Pharisaic genius that too long escaped Christian detection. The tragedy for Christians is that we have steadfastly missed the genetic connection between Jesus and the Pharisees. There is more insight into Jesus in his continuity with them than in his discontinuity (which exists on some points, but is not a radical discontinuity).

To return to my autobiographical tracings, I am further appreciative of Richard Bernstein's guidance through the scylla and charybdis of relativity and objectivity: if there is no uninterpreted fact, we are left without any way of adjudicating experience. Richard Rorty has made a huge contribution to American thought in bringing the pragmatic and hermeneutical traditions into such fruitful dialogue. William Dean has brought these same discussions into critical interaction with Jacques Derrida and deconstructionism, and has more fully historicized the nature of the theological task. It is Dean's conviction that there is no theological statement that is not in some way also an historical statement. Again I sense the God of Abraham, Isaac and Jacob; the God of Jesus, Peter, Mary, James, Martha. In the next chapter I will pick up the work of these people in greater detail. All of them are people whose projects are still being carried forward, and none of them would claim finality for his position.

To shift focus: my growing interest in empirical theology brought with it a profound respect for the role of the social sciences in theological reflection. During two years at St. John's University, my colleague, Dan Rish Finn, convoked a colloquium several times a semester between faculty of the school of theology and faculty from the social sciences. We took turns circulating papers we thought would be of interest to both disciplines, and then met over a meal to discuss the papers. This was helpful for me in two ways. First, I experienced the fruitfulness of disciplined conversation between theology and the social sciences, and saw it exemplified, e.g., how the sociology of knowledge can illuminate the formation of a doctrinal tradition.

Second, the formation of relationships that were both professional and personal was more helpful and lovely than words can acknowledge. Theologians are sometimes literate in the social sciences, but they rarely have the time to develop primary disciplined instincts in them. We have a hard time keeping abreast of developments in our own fields! But true interdisciplinary collegiality among persons of various disciplines, which is harder to bring off than most people would imagine, is a way of engaging the disciplined instincts of two or more areas of inquiry in dialogic, and sometimes dialectic conversation. When the conversation spawns community, the gift is enhanced many-fold. I acknowledge my indebtedness to a community of scholars from whose critical interaction I have profited over and over, and in this regard I am especially indebted to my friend and colleague Michael Cowan.

In the work that follows, I have made ample use of the social sciences to deepen our understandings of those historical events that carry within them intimations of ultimacy. Some of this work is mine. But I also depend often on the work of others, for example, Gerd Theissen's use of sociology to illuminate the origins of both rural[2] and urban communities[3] in Christianity's early years; or Howard Clark Kee's examination of Christian origins from a sociological perspective[4]; or Wayne Meeks' sociological assessment of Paul's world[5]; or Bruce Malina's use of cultural anthropology to examine the social world of the New Testament.[6] The list could go on and on.[7]

I must also mention an important summer trek to Israel in 1974, and then a half year in Jerusalem in 1982 while on the faculty for the Jerusalem program of St. John's University. Whitehead once spoke of "how historical tradition is handed down by the direct experience of physical surroundings."[8] Place speaks.

The friendship and encouragement of Rabbi Michael Goldberg who held the Chair of Jewish Studies at St. John's University from 1983–1985 was an important support. Thanks to a sabbatical, a research grant from St. John's, and helpful contacts from Rabbi Goldberg, I was able to spend a year at the University of Judaism in Los Angeles, and profit from the generous time and critical interaction I received from Professors Joel Rembaum and Elieser Slomovic.

I regret that I have not mastered Hebrew as I would like, nor have I systematically worked through the huge body of rabbinic materials in translation. I have tried to grapple with some of the critical tractates just to feel the character of their composition and their concerns; but for the most part I have had to rely on secondary sources by Jewish writers, among whom I note especially George Foot Moore and Ephraim Urbach. I am grateful there are such learned resources. Finally, I am aware that for one trained primarily in philosophical theology, I have had to venture far afield from my original training. I have tried to do that responsibly, but I am aware of the limitations. However, the project that this book and the succeeding volumes represent seems important enough for some foolhardy souls like myself to get into the discussion. So here I am with great tentativeness.

Much good work has been done in recent decades on the Jewishness of Christian beginnings. Sometimes the great scholars themselves see issues very differently from each other. One of my intentions throughout this work is to make some of this literature accessible, albeit in a quite second-hand way. I hope I have been reasonably faithful, and I apologize ahead of time for the lapses which I know exist.

As they say, all the rest is history.

Notes

1. Susan A. Handelman, *The Slayers of Moses: The Emergence of Rabbinic Interpretation in Modern Literary Theory* (Albany: SUNY, 1982), p. 3.

2. Gerd Theissen, *The Sociology of Early Palestinian Christianity* (Philadelphia: Fortress, 1978).

3. Gerd Theissen, *The Social Setting of Pauline Christianity* (Philadelphia: Fortress, 1982).

4. Howard Clark Kee, *Christian Origins in a Sociological Perspective* (Philadelphia: Westminster, 1980).

5. Wayne A. Meeks, *The First Urban Christians* (New Haven: Yale, 1983).

6. Bruce J. Malina, *The New Testament World* (Atlanta: John Knox, 1983).

7. For a survey of materials treating the social world of the New Testament, cf. Carolyn Osiek, *What Are They Saying About the New Testament?* (New York: Paulist, 1984).

8. Alfred North Whitehead, *Science and Philosophy* (Paterson: Littlefield, Adams, & Co., 1964), p. 12.

1

An Historicist Conversation and Some of Its Grammar

Introduction: Conversation with Jesus the Jew

Jesus was a Jew. He lived his life without remainder in the context of his Jewish faith. Whatever day that became clear to me was a day of grace. Jewish writers have long understood the utter Jewishness of Jesus. Only more recently have many Christian historians, exegetes and theologians made the same affirmation.

The disciples of Jesus during his life, and the communities that form soon after his death, do indeed have a clear identity. While this is true, they do not experience themselves as anything other than a group of Jews within Judaism, albeit with something indeed very new and very distinguishing. Yet the genuine newness they experience does not rupture their communion with Judaism. During his own life, Jesus prays and preaches regularly in the synagogue, which can only mean that he perceives himself and is perceived by peers as nothing other than fully Jewish. The post-Easter communities break bread together because it is their Christian feast (with precedents, of course, in their Jewish heritage), and they also pray regularly in the synagogue because they are Jews and belong there.

From the beginning the question of continuity and discontinuity between Jewish and Christian communities has had an urgency that regularly escaped resolution. For Christians, however, the discontinuity has been thematic since the final decades of the first century. Most christological interpretation has been "supersessionist," that is, it has interpreted Jesus as initiating a new Covenant that supersedes Judaism. Historically, it is quite improbable that Jesus had any such thing in mind.

There is little likelihood that Jesus had any conscious intention of founding a new religious institution either superseding Judaism or alongside it. If, for reasons of historical probability, we refrain from an active voice verb saying that "Jesus founded the church," Christian faith never hesitates for a moment to say that our church is founded in Jesus the Christ and in God's gift of Covenant with us in and through Jesus. Here we are again with the ghosts of continuity and discontinuity, the same ones that haunt Christianity's own sacred texts: the continuity is clearer in Mark's Gospel than in John's, in the genuine Pauline epistles than in the pseudo-Pauline pastoral letters.

Christian continuity with Jewishness is my concern in these pages. If Jesus did not step outside of Judaism to be who he was in his life, can he still be that for Christians today? What ways of interpreting his christological meaning are available to us that do not themselves step outside of Jesus' Jewishness? My goal in this book is modest. Using the resources of Jewishness likely to have been part of Jesus' own religious world, I want to have a conversation about Jesus' meaning today which honors both the Jewishness of Jesus and the faith of Christians.

In the Christian scriptures there is an abundance of very Jewish reflection upon the christological meaning of Jesus. However, a Jewish sense of things early gave way to a rather more Greek sense of things as a framework for interpreting the meaning of Jesus. After that Greek meanings often replaced Jewish meanings for the same word or expression. For example, in the synoptic Gospels the expression "Son of God" carries a very ancient Jewish meaning: someone who is chosen by God for God's work in the world. In John's later Gospel, "Son of God" implies a sonship that originates in Jesus' pre-existence. And for centuries Christians have heard a Johannine meaning for "Son of God" in Matthew or Mark. A Hellenized Christian meaning replaced a more Hebraic Christian meaning.

The Jewish road, that is, the Palestinian Jewish road, became the far less travelled road. The conversation this book undertakes is meant to be a conversation on that less travelled road. One cannot, of course, walk an ancient road today with the subjectivity of an ancient walker. Our undertaking is then an exercise in retrieval—retrieving as much as we can from another time, another place, another voice, and then, from the vantage point of life today, engaging what we have retrieved in a serious and disciplined conversation.

My interests in the retrieval of Jesus' Jewishness are not merely historical, though that is by itself a good reason. My interests have a lot to do with trying to find some salvation for a tragic relationship between Christians and Jews. A Christian reclamation of its own Jewishness would help greatly. But what an incredible richness it is for the life of Christians in today's world to repossess the remarkable instincts of Jewish faith. For a start, I think of the moving picture of a God who *truly* struggles with us in the work of creation and redemption, a God who (as Heschel said) is in search of us, a God whose success in history as God has need of us. And Jesus is *this* God's son.

A christology which resources itself in the Jewish religious world of Jesus cannot, of course, be a meta-christology which makes all other christologies coherent. One can't do that even with the christologies that co-exist in the

Christian scriptures themselves. No christology can say everything. Reality, and especially christological reality, is deeper in meaning and mystery than human word can catch. Our theologies, like our words, can do nothing more than (as Eliot said) make a raid on the inarticulate. But that is a lot. My concern is to try to honor both Jesus' Jewishness and Christian faith, not by accounting for everything, but by saying something true, and by not saying anything that violates either Jesus' Jewishness or Christian faith. What I have to say will not fully satisfy Christians or Jews, nor does it fully satisfy me. Yet I am convinced that this kind of conversation on an old and dusty road is worthy of whatever walking and talking time we commit to it.

Conversation is rarely aware of how deeply it is shaped by the grammar of the language spoken. The grammar of a language has a lot to do with not just how we speak, but with how we experience what we speak about. When I speak of the grammar of conversation in this chapter, I mean grammar in an analogous sense—some of the factors that structure how the walking and talking will proceed in this book. Before the conversation on the less travelled road gets seriously underway, I want to address some convictions about experiencing and talking about experience that underpin the entire inquiry.

The "Grammar" of the Conversation

There are three parts to the ''grammar'' of this conversation: (1) religious empiricism; (2) the metaphorical character of basic human understanding; and (3) ''conversation'' as a hermeneutical image of theological reflection.

For the empiricism, I am indebted to the philosophy of William James, especially as presented in *Essays in Radical Empiricism* and *A Pluralistic Universe.*[1] I am indebted above all to the empiricism in Alfred North Whitehead's work, especially as presented in his reflections on speculative philosophy, early in *Process and Reality.*[2]

Religious empiricism was developed at the University of Chicago Divinity School in the 1930's through the early 1960's. Henry Nelson Wieman and Bernard Meland are pioneering figures. Bernard M. Loomer has most explicitly addressed the use of Whitehead's philosophical empiricism. William Dean and Nancy Frankenberry are continuing to develop and redefine religious empiricism in the 1980's. William Dean has recently suggested that ''historicism'' probably captures the true intentionality of this movement better than ''empiricism.''[3] I think he is right. It is my hope that an historicist approach to the issues I have already named will keep christological interpretation closer to its experiential bases.

In the early pages of his opus magnum, Whitehead reminded his readers that all of his philosophical categories should be regarded as metaphors that are mutely appealing for an imaginative leap.[4] Later thinkers, and especially Paul Ricoeur, have helped us understand how metaphors mediate our primal experience and primal understanding—they are not mere embellishments of thought but belong internally and primordially to how we experience.[5] In this work I am concerned to bring out into the open the metaphorical character of Christian understandings of God as well as Christian understandings of Jesus. I want to make more visible the multiple metaphors that have been used in our religious interpretations, and the impossibility of coordinating them into a single coherent understanding.

From the perspective of hermeneutics I am recommending the advantage of thinking of both philosophy and theology as "on-going conversation." Thinking of theology and philosophy not as bodies of learning but as a disciplined sort of continuing conversation is a recognition of the time-bound, conditioned, irreducibly perspectival character of all experience, all understanding, all articulation. That is no less true of the scriptures themselves and of all religious traditions.

We are not subjects who have non-distorted, mirror-like experience of objects. There is no such thing as uninterpreted fact. Further, our interpretations always impinge upon what we call a fact. We the interpreters always get into the facts themselves! Nor are the interpretations we make merely our way of grabbing hold of past events, because how we interpret the past is also how we build the future. "Conversation" is the hermeneutical image that Hans-Georg Gadamer recommends for understanding how we experience and understand.[6] Richard Rorty has brought the empirical and hermeneutical traditions into strong dialogue.[7] Nelson Goodman makes the case for how our interpretation of the world creates the worlds we inhabit.[8] With indebtedness to Gadamer, David Tracy leads the way in appropriating "conversation" as an image for theology.[9]

A conversation on a Jewish road about the meaning of Jesus is an attempt to retrieve better some of the original voice of Jesus and his followers. As a way of interpreting a past event, it is also a way of building the future, a way of making the world.

I will take up each of these three concerns in turn.

Empiricism and the Scientific Revolution

The empirical impulse springs from the scientific revolution, and has been at work in the Western soul especially since the sixteenth century. It has taken many forms, and the ones I am most concerned with are twentieth century forms. While we can surely not equate the empirical tradition with an ancient Hebrew tradition, they are nonetheless profoundly congenial in their respect for experience, their restive patience with becoming, their affection for the historical and their comfort with the ambiguous. Theology has tended to stay clear of empiricism for reasons I will indicate. But I agree, rather, with James' assessment:

> Let empiricism once become associated with religion, as hitherto, through some strange misunderstanding, it has become associated with irreligion, and I believe that a new era of religion . . . will be ready to begin. . . . I fully believe that such an empiricism is a more natural ally than dialectics ever were, or can be, of the religious life.[10]

If empiricism has not enjoyed a very good reputation in religious circles, the reasons need to be examined and reappraised.

The scientific revolution drastically changed the Western mind's perception about how we know anything and everything. The message is: all knowledge arises out of lived experience, and lived experience is historical, particular, concrete. As Dean has summarized well:

> On empirical grounds there is no such thing as abstract knowledge; there is only concrete particular knowledge which might be generalized about. If God's novel and concrete actions are to be read, they must be read empirically, out of specific historical situations. . . . [11]

The key issue, of course, is what is meant by "experience."

"Experience" has one meaning in earlier scientific understandings and in the philosophy of the British empirical philosophies, and another meaning in James and Whitehead. The first meaning, that of sense experience, is not religiously useful, because God, if God exists, would not be the kind of reality that sense experience could register. James and Whitehead both include sense experience, but have a much more inclusive meaning for "experience." It is that meaning which is religiously useful—or rather necessary. When I speak of religious empiricism I mean this later and larger sense of experience. The radical empiricism of James, and Whitehead's similar understanding, will be our point of departure.

Let us begin with the earlier sense meaning, for that is what many people today popularly understand by "experience"—sometimes referred to as sensualist empiricism. These modes of thought presume that sense experience is where knowing begins, and that all of our knowledge is derived from it. Religious sensitivities have regularly stressed that God cannot be directly seen with eyes, heard with ears, felt with hands, etc. If this is true, then God could at best be a sort of postulate, a reasonable guess, but never an honest datum of direct experience. For that reason, theology has never seriously flirted with sensualist empiricism.

Both empiricisms have one thing in common. Each is committed to the deliverances of lived experience as the starting point of all knowing. But one account of "experience" is so much vaster than the other.

Paradigm Shift in Western Culture

Before addressing radical empiricism, I want to take a short "time out" to note how deep a cultural transformation got underway in the sixteenth century with the beginning of the scientific revolution. What has gone on in the intervening centuries, reaching a broader cultural consciousness in our own time, amounts to a seismic shift in the Western imagination. I mean the most fundamental *image* we have of how we know, and of what truth is. The earlier *image* emphasized reason as our most fundamental way of getting truth. Empiricism emphasizes immediate experience as our only initial access to truth. The empiricial tradition integrates the function of reason, but relates reason essentially to experience if it is to "tell us the truth." One consequence of this shift, for example, is the insistence that religious meanings come from the concrete human experience of God in human history. All theological meanings are therefore also historical meanings. In our reflection upon such experience we weave conceptual understandings, of course, but the logic is woven upon the experience. The "logic of God" is disallowed as a starting point.

I want to continue tracking with the paradigm shift that scientific empiricism precipitated. Until recent times, a Greek image of knowledge and truth has dominated Christian theology, and several mainstream contemporary theological movements have continued the trajectory. (In the final analysis, I believe that Karl Rahner and Bernard Lonergan are closer to the Greek imagination, even though they, and Lonergan particularly, address the importance of empiricism to theology.) The Greek imagination was a major influence upon the Western tradition, and not just upon theology, before the scientific revolution. While the Greeks certainly valued sense experience, they saw reason as the highest human faculty—and reason did not have to weave itself upon experience to tell the truth. Reason could tell the truth about reality by itself, since the order of the world is essentially and without remainder rational. Its rational order is derived from the reason (*logos*) or mind of God.

The lower mind, which knows through sense experience, can know only concrete, temporal things. The higher mind—reason—knows essences and order. Although no one ever had a sense experience of an unchanging being, one can reason, nonetheless, that perfect being cannot change. Any being that can become worse isn't perfect. And if it can become better, it's not now perfect. If it can be other than it is, then right now it isn't all that it can be. In spite of a consistent biblical intuition into God's changing relationship with us, the Greek imagination posited the immutability of God, trusting the "inexorable logic" of perfect being. There are self-evident first principles which reason knows. In contrast, the scientific imagination stresses immediate experience as the only source of understanding, and allows only those concepts whose experiential origins can be displayed.

Further, in the Greek imagination, the human mind is understood contemplatively: it is made for knowing, and finds its satisfaction in the immediate beholding of truth. Faithful to the way Greeks imagine human happiness, St. Thomas speaks of the beatific vision as our final end. It is an eternal contemplative act.

The empirical imagination stresses, rather, that knowing is for the sake of practice; it is in the service of qualitative living, not superficially but deeply. Whitehead and James both stress the function of reason in the direction of history. And the mind experiences fulfillment when it does this effectively. For Christians, Jesus is the most important clue we have to the nature of God. However, the intent of Jesus' teaching, especially his parables, is not to disclose the nature of deity, but to indicate how the daughters and sons of deity are meant to live in order for their togetherness to usher in the Reign of God. The tranformation of relationships that God's reign elicits is indeed such a marked grace in the quality of life that people named the Jesus-event "Good News." Too often "Gospel" or "Godspel" has lost the exuberance that belongs to truly good news, and just names a book. Jewish sensibilities are nearer an empirical than a rational temper.

In the empirical framework, the starting point is *experience of the world* and the finishing point is *experience in the world. Saeculum* is one of the Latin words for world. The empirical imagination has rightly been called "secular" because of the primacy given to the world in our image of human experience and human understanding. Religious empiricism stresses the experience of God in and through the world. The Hebrew "report" upon God is woven of the historical events in which God is experienced. The tendency to contrast "religious" with "secular" stresses, I am convinced, not "religious" with "non-religious" so much as Greek imagination with empirical imagination.

"Experience" in Radical Empiricism

I want to turn now to radical empiricism. It is not difficult to understand why religious thought was suspicious of an earlier empiricism that gave primordial status to sense experience. Radical empiricism holds that sense experience is not primordial at all. It is rather a kind of "late abstraction" from much larger, fuller, richer, and not too manageable experience. Radical empiricism is concerned with the full range of historical experience, the depth, the breadth and the incredible relational complexity of all that which is the womb of our becoming. James and Whitehead use expressions like "pure experience" and "raw experience" to catch the more massive sweep of our primal experience. Some examples will help.

A person, at any given moment, is the outcome of an incredible welter of experience. My history began very long ago. The specifically human form of existence that I experience has been in the making for a million years and more. Small organic transformations have been going on all the while which, through bodies, get transmitted from one generation to the next. Even further back, the state of the earth (temperature, moisture, etc.) had to have a certain shape before organisms could emerge. That shape depended not just upon the earth, but upon the sun, upon the other planets in the solar system, upon the relation of the solar system to other parts of our galaxy, upon the relation of our not terribly significant galaxy to still further reaches of the cosmos. There is a causal interconnectedness of all those factors, and real effects get transmitted from one entity to another. Energies that first pulsed billions of years ago still reverberate. The full identity of any human being upon this earth cannot neglect the multifariousness of that teeming matrix of causal influences. We are all of that. That past remains, and it remains precisely through the present moment's experience of it.

Or again: to understand my present experience, I must reckon with the fact that English is my native language, and that language shapes experience in fundamental ways. My language today must reckon causally with Anglo-Saxon. It must reckon with the Roman influence upon the British Isles and the consequent influence of Latin upon English. Julius Caesar is on all English speaking tongues, but sense perception doesn't register his presence. Anglo-Saxon roots must reckon with their older emergence from pristine Teutonic forms. The gods of the north created different "earths" than the gods of the south, and the different earths got different words. Still further back, the Indo-European linguistic structures differ in some radical ways from Semitic structures; and we know of course that grammatical structures impinge profoundly upon perceptual structures. All those factors truly are part of what goes into my accounting for exactly who I am at this moment. All of this causal input is received by the organism, is "felt" primally, has essential effects, but escapes sense perception in the main. The concept of experience that I am presupposing includes all of these "felt" effects, even though they are not felt consciously or sensually.

When we consider all the impulses that surge through us to make us who we are, it is but a very small amount of the massive, vague, raw experience that registers as sense experience. Sense experience is selective, clear and distinct—in a word, it is abstract. Dean suggests the image of the Hebrews in the wilderness as closer to raw experience: "that unformed, uninterpreted, physical cacophony of emotional, valuational, largely unconscious and in every sense ambiguous, objective experience, felt initially and blindly by the body."[12] I want to be clear: when I speak of religious empiricism, I do not mean sense experience, but the richer, though less manageable, yield of raw experience. I do not underestimate the insight into primal experience that can come from sense experience and from reasoning woven upon sense experience. But I want to affirm that sense experience is not the kind of experience in which religious empiricism is grounded.

Empiricism/Historicism

Another way of describing the empirical situation is to stress the historical nature of all experience. We exist in the world in our bodies. We exist in the world in time. We can only know what is related to us in the world and is together with us in time. To claim to experience God is also, therefore, to claim that God is in the world with us, and that God, therefore, is truly historical. Again, to follow Dean, the empirical historicist holds that the religious subject and the religious object are both historical.[13] In classical theism, the religious object (God) is not historical. God is interpreted as essentially non-temporal. The biblical experience witnesses to the contrary: God is an essential component of the evolving history of the Jewish people. But equally, Jewish history is a real component of the experience of God, which is to say, of the concrete reality of God. The specific action of God in history is the datum for theology. Religious empiricism would hold that theological reasoning must never "wonder" away from the historical action of God from which it arises. There should be no logic about God that is detatched from the data of concrete religious experience.

A radical empiricism never presupposes that a concrete experience of anything or anyone is an exhaustive experience. Nor, therefore, do we conclude that the specific action of God experienced in the world is a full disclosure of divine reality. Even so, the only disclosures we do have are the specific historical presences of God in our lives. Empirical theology insists that we make no claims beyond what the historical experience of God elicits. It is an empirical/historicist commitment to keep visible and articulate the connection between historical meaning and theological meaning. As I hope to show, especially in the second volume, expressions like Covenant, Holy Spirit, Word of God, Son of God, Christ, etc., are interpretations of historical events. When we interpret what these words and expressions mean, we must put on display the concrete events that warrant the interpretation. This empirical/historicist procedure is methodologically intrinsic to establishing theological meaning. Putting such events on display makes for longer theological treatises; but they have more stories!

Part of the modesty of religious empiricism is its historicism: it respects the historicity of human experience, and limits its claims, even about God, to what has a referent somewhere, sometime, in immediate lived experience. It never claims to make more than a partial statement, though it may be utterly convinced of its limited truth. A second reason for modesty is the inaccessibility of any object of experience to total experience. We never experience another in its fullness. The richer the being, the more each disclosure intimates its fuller reaches—but also the unreachability of its fullness. *The mystery of being is not in its otherness, but in the inexhaustibility of its hereness.* Especially God!

What we behold, in Whitehead's words, is "the whole universe in the process of attainment."[14] Because of the interdependence of all parts of the universe, "any local agitation shapes the whole universe. The distant effects are minute, but they are there."[15] In "The Kingdom of God Is Within You," Francis Thompson made poetry of our inter-connectedness:

> The angels keep their ancient places;—
> Turn but a stone, and start a wing!
> 'Tis ye, 'tis your estranged faces,
> That miss the Many Splendored thing.

A kicked pebble sets an angel's wing aflutter.

Alan Watts hints at the unmanageability of the total data involved in even the tiniest event: "We can never, never describe *all* the features of the total situation, not only because every situation is infinitely complex, but also because the *total* situation is the universe."[16] Similarly, empirical theologian Bernard Meland observes that since "relations extend every event indefinitely . . . the very phrase 'exact knowledge' is but a manner of speaking."[17] When religious empiricism commits itself to the deliverances of experience, it intends a very large understanding of experience. What an entity "experiences" is the totality of causal pulses that account in small and large ways for its identity: all its relations, all its moods, all its reasons, all its choices. All its everything! One reason for the partial opaqueness of all experience is the inexhaustible complexity of reality itself.

The partial opaqueness of human understanding also has to do with what it means to be an embodied (in-body-ed) subject of experience. In a recent study of Jewish experience, Michael Wyschogrod calls Israel's reason "a dark reason," because of its embodied character.[18] But everyone's reason is a dark reason because we are alike in this; it is only perhaps that the Jewish temperament has better seen the situation. All our bodily processes have a most vital bearing on well-being, including consciousness. Yet those processes remain, for the most part, opaque to our direct knowledge. We are in the dark about most of what our bodies are doing at any given moment.

Human consciousness is therefore always an upsurge from the darkness of a body not fully understood by the consciousness that resides in the body. . . . Embodied consciousness is human consciousness. It is consciousness surrounded by darkness, and not only with respect to its object but also in terms of its own being. The darkness of the body, the fact that it is the dwelling place of consciousness but never fully illuminated by it, confers on human consciousness its uniqueness. It counterbalances and corrects the thrust of human consciousness toward autonomy. . . . [19]

Wyschogrod feels that Jewish respect for the body accounts for its awareness that its reason is a dark reason. It is dark because so many regions of the body's full experience are never direct data for sense experience and for consciousness. The bodily home of human consciousness is itself partly in the dark, which cannot but deeply condition the functions of consciousness. If theological meanings are also historical meanings, then we must be respectful of theological opaqueness, and be willing to let it alone. This is not to be tolerant of muddleheadedness—only to honor the conditioned nature of human understanding. The tolerance of unclarity that is recommended belongs not to the beginning of knowing, but at the far end of inquiry, when we have exhausted the clear knowables. Tolerance at this point is honor paid to the mystery of being, and not just capitulation to the limits of the knowing subject. The foundations of ambiguity are "out there" just as much as "in here."

Events are laden. They are heavy with a thousand causes. They are luminous with a thousand references. They laugh or cry with a thousand feelings.

Sense perception is but a particular way in which a small selection of causal data registers in entities equipped with a nervous system and a brain. That selective focus may not be inaccurate, but it is a partial picture. Sense perceptions represent a few pieces of data abstracted from the whole. They repeatedly trick our human responses by their appeal of clarity and distinctness into believing that they have disclosed everything. Philosophy and theology are especially prone to play the same trick on us because they appear to tell the whole truth.

The total relational web of causal influences at work in an entity's emergence always forms a "shadowy background" for the selected details that emerge with more clarity as sense perceptions. Whitehead and Meland describe those shadows with expressions like "the penumbral regions," or "the adumbrative character" of reality. Both rightly insist that vague and shadowy experience is not less real because of its indistinctness, but fuller, richer, more immediate and more complete. It is "pure experience" that is concrete rather than sense experience which abstracts from the total event, or consciousness which abstracts still further.

If it is a small part of the total picture that registers in the form of sense perception, it is a still smaller part that is finally clothed with consciousness. And only some part of consciousness is conceptualized and reasoned about. Our reasoning allows us to discern patterns, to make generalizations, to gain some measure of control and predictability. "Rationality is assured," Meland comments, "because events have a structure"; and Meland's typical qualifying "but" follows: "but the events are known to have adumbration as well, which fact tempers the impact of rationality as a clue to the world's meaning."[20] This is a considerable reversal of our normal sense of things. We usually feel that the clear and distinct deliverances of sense experience are very concrete, and that dim apprehensions and vagueness in view of complexity are abstract. But it is rather the elusive fullness that is concrete, and the clear and distinct that is abstract. That part of sense perception that rises to consciousness is even further removed from concreteness, and therefore more abstract. This understanding certainly does not devalue the functions of conscious reason—civilization is based upon the adventures of humankind's great and large ideas. However, we must never forget where concreteness really lies!

No concrete reality in its totality, in all its messy and elusive fullness, can be grasped without remainder by sense perception or by consciousness. James wrote: "The word 'and' trails along after every sentence. Something always escapes. 'Ever not quite' has to be said of the best attempts made anywhere in the universe at attaining all inclusiveness."[21] Sense perceptions are the means whereby a concrete entity makes its appearance to consciousness and reason.

Whitehead contrasts the final Appearance of something to conscious awareness with its initial Reality (the full event in all its concreteness):

Consciousness is the weapon that strengthens the artificiality of an occasion
of experience. It raises the importance of the final Appearance relatively to
that of the initial Reality. Thus it is Appearance which in consciousness is
clear and distinct, and it is Reality which lies dimly in the background with
its details hardly to be distinguished in consciousness. What leaps into conscious attention is a mass of presuppositions about Reality rather than intuitions of Reality itself. It is here that liability to error arises. The
deliverances of clear and distinct consciousness require criticism by references to elements which are neither clear nor distinct. On the contrary, they
are dim, massive, and important. These dim elements provide for art that
final background of tone apart from which its effects fade. The type of Truth
which human art seeks lies in the eliciting of this background to haunt the
object presented for clear consciousness.[22]

The kind of empiricism I am recommending to theology is one that is based in
experience, when experience means both the "messy" and "vague" initial
experience of reality, and its "filtered" appearance to consciousness through
sense data. Sense perceptions are clues to what Whitehead calls the initial
Reality. They are symbols of it, if you will, and therefore critically important.
They are symbols because they participate in the larger reality to which they
point.

Empiricism equally prizes conscious awareness. There is a clean beauty
in coherent understanding, a commanding power in accurate, generalized, abstract conceptualizations. Without them human civilization could not exist.
But these systematic understandings, as Whitehead says, always require criticism by reference to elements which are neither clear nor distinct. For theology, these self-correcting critical references are to the great "motifs" of our
sacred literature, to our symbols and metaphors, to our rituals and our prized
stories. Poetic elements are too often introduced into theological discourse to
elucidate a technical point. Rather, we range closer to the richness of pure religious experience when theology functions to elucidate for us our foundational
religious metaphors. Metaphor is not ornament. It is essential thinking and
speaking about the mystery of concreteness.

Religious Empiricism

Theology will always, because it is a particular kind of consciousness,
strengthen the artificiality of our religious experience. In this context, artifi-

ciality must not be taken in a pejorative sense. It means rather that some "artifice" has been used to help reconstruct an initial Reality laden with religious content. It is in such reconstruction that religious meanings emerge and values begin to clothe our perception. Theology, like all systematic reflection, unlevels the experiential terrain by singling out some features as more notable and important than others, creating new kinds of importance. The energies of life are directed to important concerns. The artificiality of theological categories can be an amazing resource for the specification of importance. The lifting up of importance alters the terrain and unflattens the horizon. The challenge is to have the benefit of rational consciousness without losing the richness and concreteness of the initial Reality. Concreteness lies with the vague, not with the clear!

The British empiricists held that things could be directly experienced, but not relationships, for none of the five senses could have relationship as a datum. They thought we could only posit relationship. The radical empirical position understands that connectedness itself is experienced. We experience that we came from somewhere. We know we are derived from a past. We are connected to something before us. It is through our bodies that we sense our causal derivation. The world is present to every person through the bodily reception of causal energies from it. Prior to any sense experience, an entity "feels" its derivation from a huge prior world. It is a bodily intuition. This bodily intuition into our essential relatedness, raised to some consciousness, is the foundational intuition that leads Whitehead to call his philosophy "the philosophy of organism."

Process religious thinkers like Bernard Meland and Bernard Loomer have tried to capture this sense of reality with "web" language. What the word "world" or "universe" or "cosmos" or "reality" denominates is a "relational web," the organic interconnectedness of all things. Each entity is a focal point in the web. It is Whitehead's presupposition (here he differs radically with Hume) that relatedness is a datum of experience, in fact, the fundamental datum. Causal interconnectedness is the starting point of experience. What we can know, whether intuitively or perceptually or conceptually, must originate in what is given to us in relationship. Period! What "period" means is: no exception. What "no exception" means is: this also counts for the human experience of God.

All we ever have is our own immediate lived experience. We do indeed profit and learn from the experience that others have. Tradition is one of the most important instances of our experience of the experience of others. Biological inheritance is one instance of an experiential trajectory: genetic code gathers and transmits experience. Culture and tradition are further examples of our experience of the experience of others. In order to be affected by the experience of others we must have *our* experience of *their* experience, which means, of course, our interpretation of their experience. Culture, like genetic code, gathers, generalizes, and transmits shared interpretations of experience. Tradition's intention is to convey experience. However, as Heidegger once warned, tradition tends to hand experience over to self-evidence, and then to block our access to the primordial sources from which our ideas were drawn.[23] The point is that when we consciously consult experience, we must not merely consult our personal lives; we also look to our interpretations and valuations of the experience of others.

If God is present to our experience it can only be on the basis of God's immanence in the immediacies of lived experience, as Bernard Meland says, "at the vortices of human experience where . . . ultimacy and immediacy traffic together."[24] Theology observes, interprets, generalizes, and then talks about this traffic. Theology is interested, therefore, in where the traffic between ultimacy and immediacy occurs.

Whitehead and Meland both sense that ultimacy is most apt to be touched at those depths of experience where our relationship with the world is most concretely actual. It is in our massive interconnectedness with the world that ultimate things are "felt"—and by "felt" I mean simply our reception of impulses from that seething, vast, causally efficacious world. I learn there, for example, that I did not make myself, that I come out of a world that pre-existed me and gave me my reality. In short, I learn there that I am a "derived" entity, and that I am finite. If we know our finitude at the level of religious experience, we have felt it primordially; we have not deduced it from logic nor induced it from sense data. At these most concrete though elusive places of contact with the world are found our better intimations about the traffic between immediacy and ultimacy.

If the philosophy of art must begin, as Suzanne Langer insists, in the art studio and not in the art museum, then theology must be initiated by those who have got caught in the traffic between immediacy and ultimacy, and not just in the formulations of other people who were in the traffic. Peter Berger's sense of inductive theology is similar: we must always begin with ordinary, daily experience. It is there that we find "signals of transcendence." These then can move to religious affirmations.[25] Similarly, Piet Schoonenberg indicates his conviction that trinitarian reflection must begin with what is known of God from God's immanence in history: theology always moves from the world to God and never in the opposite direction.[26] "The world" here means for Schoonenberg, as it does for Hebrew experience, a world in which ultimacy is intuited to be at work.

The worldly presences of God are the data of theology. Religious empiricism can be stated that simply. The world, then, must never disappear from discourse about God. This is one clear reason for the historicist nature of theological reflection.

The immanence of God is theology's province. Immanence and transcendence are coordinate terms. Every entity/person is *more than* any self-communication presents. Every entity/person is *more than* all self-communications taken together could present. Yet there are no clues at all to the *more than* except in the concreteness of self-communication, and what can be surmised or intuited on the basis of it. "Otherness," or transcendence, is known about always and only through "withness." "Withness" always carries intimations of "otherness." There is no such thing as "totally other" any more than "totally immanent."

Whiteheadian Empiricism: An Image

In *Process and Reality,* Whitehead offers an image for how empirical philosophy proceeds, an image apt for empirical theology as well.

> The true method of discovery is like the flight of an aeroplane. It starts from the ground of particular observation; it makes a flight into the thin air of imaginative generalization; and it again lands for renewed observation rendered acute by rational interpretation.[27]

Let us examine each part of this tri-partite pattern.

To begin from the ground of particular observation is to note our lived experience as accurately as we can. We describe it as best we can, with an awareness that every "fact" is an interpreted fact—granting that we always interpret. Our first stage commitment is to stay with particular facts.

When we have gathered together multiple facts of lived experience whose character suggests some commonality, we then move into part two: the descriptive generalization of experience. Now we have begun a process of deliberate abstraction. This generalization, of course, involves even more interpretation. When we are deeply impressed by elements of commonality, and when we find our understanding enlivened by generalized insight, we often weave together systems of generalized interpretation. All philosophical and theological systems are imaginative generalizations (or should be!) of accumulated lived experience. Sometimes the imaginative generalizations are given very abstract names. What new student of Aristotle has not been fascinated with matter, form, act, potency, formal, material, efficient and final causality. What new student of Heidegger hasn't revelled in *Dasein* and *Existentiell*. What new devotee of Whitehead hasn't played with "hybrid physical prehensions" and "non-conformal propositions." Imaginative generalization is an extension of descriptive generalization, because it means taking a descriptive generalization and stretching it imaginatively beyond its original point of origin. Here we usually take words we already know and stretch their meanings beyond those we first found them with. When terribly hard pressed, we make new words.

Some imaginative generalizations are done with far more concrete images. In volume II, I will indicate how Hebrew words like "Covenant," "Spirit," "Word," "Heart," etc., are generalizations of particular religious experiences. Our best understanding of what these words mean comes from gaining as much access as possible to the particular places where ultimacy and immediacy met and were thus described, and to see how these same understandings helped Israel continue to create her history with God.

The stage of generalization and imaginative description is a rational stage. It's where we bring our best gifts of reason to bear. This is the stage where we begin to ask questions like this: if this is true, then mustn't this second thing be true also? If both of these seem true, then doesn't that shed new light on how we'd better understand this third area of experience? We rightly expect our interpretive schemas to be coherent. We do, by and large, feel that things are "together," not totally perhaps, but reasonably. We encounter sufficient ambiguity, and enough places where logic runs out, to keep our own interpretive schemas under some measure of suspicion. However, our concern for the coherence of our systems of thought is not misplaced. Only *ultimate* trust in them would be misplaced. Our massive generalized insights are our large ideas, our seminal grand intuitions, the root metaphors upon which our worlds are constructed, our civilizations conceived and nurtured. Our splendor as human beings is often witnessed by what we achieve during our flights into the thin air of imaginative generalization.

Stage three of Whitehead's empiricism is the flight's return to the landing field. The *raison d'être* for the imaginative scheme is the elucidation of immediate experience, which Whitehead insists is the sole justification for any system of thought.[28] Therefore, we bring the categories of understanding we have fashioned in the air back to the ground of experience to check them out. We got some distance from historical particulars to fashion our systematic understandings, and now we must renew intercourse with particulars. If our generalizations are indeed insightful, then our experience will be "rendered acute by rational interpretation."

As this book unfolds, I hope to retrieve some interpretations of God that are likely to have been part of the religious world in which Jesus lived. I will follow the empirical procedure outlined here. That involves a long look at particular experiences before generalizations are made. Theological generalizations must be grounded in thick historical experience. We then look at the ways in which the ancient Hebrews used metaphor to generalize their significant religious history. Finally, using these singularly Jewish flights into the thin air of imaginative generalization, we will examine whether or not some of our contemporary Christian experience is rendered acute by our rational interpretation.

I want to insist at this point that empirical and rational are integrally conjoined in the philosophical method of Whitehead. About this he is much clearer than William James. If I stress the word "empirical," it is because methodologically we are committed to beginning and ending in experience. But the rational contribution is integral to our experiential commitment, and is, indeed, a mode of experience.

The empiricism of James, like that of Whitehead, begins with pieces and parts and their relationships. Whatever patterns we name are those (and only those) discerned in and among the pieces and parts. Though James does not stress the partnership that should obtain between empiricism and rationalism, he nonetheless clarifies the deductive epistemology that is also Whitehead's:

> Empiricism is known as the opposite of rationalism. Rationalism tends to emphasize universals and to make wholes prior to parts in the order of logic as well as in that of being. Empiricism, on the contrary, lays the explanatory stress upon the part, the element, and treats the whole as a collection and the universal as an abstraction. My description of things, accordingly, starts with the parts and makes of the whole a being of the second order. It is essentially a mosaic philosophy, a philosophy of plural facts. . . . [29]

This kind of empiricism, adjusted to theological concerns, conditions the christology that is being developed in this project. It is a christology of plural facts. I want to elaborate briefly on this.

Alan Watts observed that it is more accurate to say we come "out of the world," rather than "into the world."[30] At the beginning of this chapter I indicated what I believe to be the thoroughgoing Jewishness of Jesus. I am interested in the Jewish world that he came "out of." A Jewish world must be presupposed for whatever identity Jesus had. The theological empiricism of this work requires that we begin with the major parts and pieces of the Jewish world out of which Jesus came religiously and culturally. We will try to put them together into a mosaic christology of plural facts. I will be working from parts toward a whole, but the whole will be of a theologically mosaic kind, not the orderly whole of seamless logic—actually more of a theomosaic than a theologic. It is my intention to avoid any theological generalization whose origination out of lived experience cannot be indicated. I am especially interested in the lived experience of the Jewish world that was a lifelong womb for the becoming of Jesus' identity.

Our theoretical systems do not only interpret the past and elucidate the present. They participate in the construction of the future. I will return to this in a later section in this chapter on hermeneutics, but it is also a theme to be noted in the empiricism of Whitehead and James and of their predecessor Charles Sanders Peirce.

Whitehead did not articulate the constructive character of interpretation as clearly as James, nor as circumspectly as Heidegger and later hermeneutical philosophers. He does, however, indicate how abstract ideas make a difference for the future: generic ideas "should make it easier to conceive of the infinite variety of specific instances which rest unrealized in the womb of nature."[31] It is clear from Whitehead's analysis of the function of reason, that reason serves to enhance the richness of our historical existence, especially by pointing us to possibilities that mean a "more" for our lives. Our more imaginative schemas do this best. Even though our systems are a response to direct observation, in a truly imaginative schema we find "imagination far outrunning the direct observations."[32] It is the essence of such speculation that it transcends immediate fact. Its business is to make thought creative of the future.[33] Although the specific language is not Whitehead's, it is also clear to him that the speculative schemas we have already formed condition our interpretation of new experience. In that sense, schemas not only help construct new fact, they engage in the reconstruction of past fact. One need only think of the many ways in which dogma and systematic theology have influenced our interpretation of the life of Jesus. For example, supersessionist christologies (which virtually dominate the doctrinal tradition) all interpret the community of disciples as a new institution that supersedes an old institution, as the expressions "Old" Testament and "New" Testament witness.

To lay out further the empirical sense of the influence of ideas on behaviors, I turn to Charles Sanders Peirce and William James on this issue. Ideas have consequences, and what ideas mean is intrinsically inclusive of their consequences. Thought produces habits of action, Peirce concluded, and the best way to make our ideas clear is to show what habits of action they spawn.[34] James developed the insight in his own way. In his essay, "What Pragmatism Means," James cites a Leipzig chemist: "All realities influence our practice, and that influence is their meaning for us."[35] James' own pragmatic formulation is clear and to the point: "There can *be* no difference anywhere that doesn't *make* a difference elsewhere—no difference in abstract truth that doesn't express itself in a difference in concrete fact and in conduct consequent upon that fact, imposed on somebody, somehow, somewhere, and somewhen."[36]

I have indicated my conviction that Jesus is an utterly Jewish fact. That conviction, if it means anything, has consequences for Christian existence, somehow, somewhere, somewhen. The differences that it makes are integral to the meaning of the phrase, "the Jewishness of Jesus." One such difference would have to be a profound transformation of Christian attitudes/behaviors toward Jews, beginning with the Jews who are Jesus' contemporaries, but most especially with our own contemporaries. We would have to reckon with the Holocaust in new ways: not only our complicity in what centuries of Christian antisemitism made possible, but as people who begin to recognize that they have devastated *their own* Jewishness. Another consequence of the recovered Jewishness of Jesus would be a pervasively historicized agenda for the Christian people of God—certainly a contrast with mainstream Christian preoccupation with a metahistorical reign of God.

Metaphorical Theology

In the lived experience of the ancient Hebrews, there is no question about God's active presence in history. God has expectations of them, which they feel are made clear to them by God. In turn, the promise of God generates return expectations on their part. There is a bi-partisan agreement. There is another experience of bi-partisan agreements to which the ancient Hebrews have recourse to interpret their relationship with God.

One of the bi-partisan agreements that make daily civil life work in the ancient world is the treaty covenant between nations. Treaty covenants are vital to peace. They create the foreign policies that govern expectations, rights and duties. When they are observed, they presumably create the conditions that favor peace and prosperity. "Covenant" becomes the generalization for the Hebrew experience of this favorable, agreement-based reciprocity between God and themselves. Many ceremonies that accompany making and enforcing treaties begin to have their religious counterparts between God and the covenanted people. The covenant metaphor then generates a system of ideas, each of which has consequences in Jewish religious behaviors, such as the periodic reading of the terms of the covenant, i.e., the Law. When something that is expected in the view of the covenant does not occur, the conclusion can only be either that God falls short of his promise, or that God's people are unworthy.

God's people, believing in God's fidelity, naturally ask: "What have we done wrong? Let us repent."

Covenant is a metaphor. The primary place where there is an immediate lived experience of covenant is the way that relationships between nations are structured in the ancient Middle East. Some of those familiar meanings are transferable to the structure of Hebrew religious experience. Yet the relationship with God is not in all ways identical, without remainder, to civil treaty covenants. God does not have a "place" with geographical boundaries. God does not raise an army and march through any country. Covenant is a key to understanding how God and the Hebrew people are related. It tells the truth because of a real similarity. Yet one must always secretly remember that in some ways the relationship between God and these people is *not* like a covenant.

Covenant is not a metaphor in the sense simply that one might become very excited about an event, and use poetic metaphor quite self-consciously to ornament that event's exquisiteness. Covenant is a fundamental understanding of what it means to be human. It is a metaphor that actually helps construct the project of being human. Covenant redescribes past experience, constructs present experience, and projects life forward into tomorrow, next year, and until the end of time. Projection, like construction of the present moment, is also a form of worldmaking. With our basic metaphors we *make* the worlds of meaning we inhabit now and shall inhabit in the future.

In her work on metaphorical theology, Sally McFague (reflecting Paul Ricoeur on this issue) observes that "metaphorical thinking constitutes the basis of human thought and language."[37] All our knowing involves the recognition of elements of sameness and elements of difference. The samenesses that allow us to make connections function metaphorically. The identification of samenesses that allows for understandings of one thing to transfer to understandings of another thing keeps language humanly manageable. We could not possibly have a proper word for every single event and entity. "This is a deficiency and lack for which we should be grateful (Ricoeur citing Boileau and Dumarsais) for if we had as many words as ideas, 'what memory would be sufficient to learn so many words, and to retain and reproduce them?' "[38]

Metaphor depends upon the fact that entity One resembles entity Two. That resemblance is manifested when a name from One is used for Two. But if Two is like One, it is also *not* like One. McFague says that metaphorical statements "always contain the whisper, 'it is *and it is not*.' "[39] For example, subjectivity is a psychological term. When Whitehead uses "subjectivity," to interpret an electron, it is relatively clear to most people that there is also the "secret 'is not.' " Even so, there is a tendency to forget that philosophical categories are interpretive language, and to treat the categories as if they were proper words for discrete entities. Whitehead calls this the fallacy of misplaced concreteness. There is the same danger for metaphorical language: to forget the "is not." Ricoeur calls it an ontological naiveté when the implicit "is not" is ignored.[40]

Theology is often prone to ontological naiveté. We forget so easily that "nature," "person," "substance," etc., are metaphors that interpret our experience of God. Throughout this work, for example, I understand *Ruach*/Spirit and *Dabhar*/Word to be metaphors that interpret our experience of God. But I intend to use them as interpretive redescriptions of experience, not as proper names originating for the purpose of naming God. They tell the truth. But there is always a critical "is not."

Every metaphor's "is not" preserves the mystery of being, whether of electrons or of deity. If forgetting the "is not" is apt to generate an ontological naiveté, dwelling too intently upon the "is not" is equally destructive of metaphorical meaning. If we pay constant attention to the "is not," we begin to make the metaphor feel like a mere "as if" instead of a strong, positive, direct insight.[41] There is then a certain kind of metaphorical naiveté required to make theological discourse work: we must genuinely know about the "is not's", and yet pass over them in secret silence, without forgetting what we know.

Thus far I have spoken about metaphors mostly as if they stood somewhat alone and discrete in their redescriptive and interpretive services. But metaphors tend to be like ideas—they exist and function in a system. If you tamper with part of the system, you tamper with the system. If you invoke part of the system in metaphor, it is likely that you buy more of the system than you realize. "The referential function," Ricoeur writes, "should be carried by a metaphoric network rather than by an isolated metaphoric statement."[42] For example, when God begins to be called Father in the Hebrew tradition, the system where the word father occurs in lived experience is a patriarchal system. It may be that the intended resemblance had to do with any good father's fidelity and care. Yet to call God "father" unavoidably reinforces the patriarchal system and its functioning behavioral norms. The male father figure is the power figure. Therefore, it is natural to import "power and might" terminology from the patriarchical system into God talk. And if we are to be holy as God is holy, we re-patriate (a not amusing pun) patriarchy right back into the construction of human experience and the projection of its possibilities.

The title "Christ Liberator" currently popular in South America interprets Jesus primarily for those fighting oppressive establishments. "Christ Liberator" is rooted in scripture, of course. But in this instance "liberator" is also evoked out of Latin America's own history. "Christ Liberator's" consequences for lived experience cannot but tap subtly into Simon Bolivar and Che Guevara meanings, since these meanings occur in the liberation metaphor system of referents. One doesn't buy into the total systems evoked by liberation images, but those systems are there and their meanings inundate liberation christology.

I am not saying that this phenomenon is wrong; it is, in fact, natural. Metaphors are not likely to have their balance corrected by calling attention to their "is not's" but rather by the counterbalance of other metaphors. It is important in God talk to keep a plethora of metaphoric systems interpretively alive.

What Hans-Georg Gadamer says about words is similar and applicable to metaphor: "every word breaks forth as if from a center and is related to a whole, through which alone it is a word. Every word causes the whole of the language to which it belongs to resonate and the whole view of the world which lies behind it to appear."[43] Every metaphor which is part of a system tends to make the whole system appear when used. This phenomenon is seldom transparent to consciousness.

The first, literal meaning of a metaphor stands in a system of meanings. And it tends to bring some of its system along with it into the second or symbolic level. Because a metaphor carries a new meaning as well, it also breaks out of the first literal meaning, and it can dart beyond its first meaning. However, I want to attend now to the power that a metaphor has to create a new system (which christological metaphors easily do). A few comments from Czech writer Milan Kundera's *The Unbearable Lightness of Being* is a good place to begin. The relationship between Tomas and Tereza is central to the novel. Early in the story Tomas looks upon Tereza who is asleep:

> . . . it occurred to him that Tereza was a child put in a pitch-daubed basket and sent downstream. He couldn't very well let a basket with a child float down a stormy river! If the Pharaoh's daughter hadn't snatched little Moses from the waves, there would have been no Old Testament, no civilization as we now know it! How many ancient myths begin with the rescue of an abandoned child! If Polybus hadn't taken in the young Oedipus, Sophocles wouldn't have written his most beautiful tragedy!
>
> Tomas did not realize at the time that metaphors are dangerous. Metaphors are not to be trifled with. A single metaphor can give birth to love.[44]

If Tomas does not merely think of Tereza as little Moses in a once and passing way, but rather consistently relates to her as the abandoned child, then the unfolding of his entire relationship with her will be conditioned by the metaphor. How their story unfolds will be shaped by the metaphor. If he is forever the rescuer of the needy child, Tomas and Tereza will never meet as equals. That is why metaphors are dangerous and not to be trifled with: a whole narrative structure can be rooted in a powerful metaphor. A metaphor fertile enough to spawn a life story is a root metaphor.

Later in the novel, Kundera again steps out of the narrative to explain how his characters are born:

> And once more I see him the way he appeared to me at the very beginning of the novel: standing at the window and staring across the courtyard at the walls opposite.

> This is the image from which he was born. As I have pointed out before, characters are not born like people, of woman; they are born of a situation, a sentence, a metaphor containing in a nutshell a basic human possibility that the author thinks no one else has discovered or said something essential about.[45]

It is well said: a root metaphor contains in a nutshell a basic human possibility. A root metaphor projects a story out in front of it. When a metaphor interprets a past or present experience, it makes a world-that-could-be stand up out there in front of the interpreter(s).

I will oversimplify the point of this book for a moment. Of the many New Testament metaphors that interpret Jesus christologically, one has dominated Christianity's unfolding self-understanding: the *Logos*/Word made flesh. For socio-cultural reasons, *Logos* was undoubtedly the best root metaphor for making the Christian story stand up there in front of Hellenized men and women, and for calling them into discipleship. However, *Logos* is almost certainly not a metaphor in Jesus' own self-understanding, as I hope to indicate. While we cannot get inside his subjectivity, we can surmise that *Logos* is not in the assumptive world of a Galilean Jew in Jesus' time.

It is worth returning to an early historical crossroads to retrieve some christological metaphors that did not spin out a Christian narrative, at least not the way a root metaphor can structure a deep story out of which people live. If the christological undertaking of this book is valuable, the reason is not merely because some very early resources that belong properly to the religious world of Jesus have been used. What would justify the project is that the less travelled but legitimate road leads to a valid Christian interpretation that is redemptive for our age.

Hermeneutics

In Greek mythology, Hermes is the lesser god who delivers the messages of Zeus to human beings, and is the patron god of messengers. Hermeneutics is aptly named after Hermes. It is about the role of interpretation in forming and delivering the messages of experience to human consciousness. One of the conclusions of historical consciousness is that there is no such thing as an uninterpreted fact. It was Nietzsche who first put it that way. Perhaps wise people over the ages have long known that when we talk about experience, we shape our talking by our own past experience, by our own vested interests, by our own language, etc., that is, we interpret. However, the postmodern, more radically historicized understanding of interpretation insists, like Einstein, that the observer has effects on the observed. "Object" is a word whose meaning presupposes an experiencing "subject." Subject and object are coordinate terms, presupposing each other for their respective meaning. There is no subject who experiences an object without interpretation being part of the experience. "Pure objectivity" becomes a contradiction in terms, because the meaning of "object" presupposes the meaning of "subject," and an experiencing subject always interprets the object. Thus interpretation always becomes an *internal* part of a "fact." Interpretation enters into the construction of fact. We are back to this paragraph's opening sentence: there is no such thing as an uninterpreted fact.

The alternative to pure objectivity is not sheer relativity. As Dean points out, there is always some element of relativity because interpretation involves some elements of free construction of what we receive into our experience. The free construction is not a conscious act. It is not a deliberate fiction, or even a fiction at all. It is the shaping of experience on the basis of all one brings from the past to the present moment. If there is some free construction, it is also true that our interpretation is never simply arbitrary, for it is based on and limited by what our experience receives, i.e., by the object of experience.[46]

Heisenberg's principle of indeterminacy has an almost historicist application. You cannot pin "fact" down to total objective accuracy. Nor can you attribute "fact" to the mere conjuring activity of an experiencing subject. What you can do is locate "fact," as it were, "within range" between objectivism and relativism.

The way in which interpretation always impinges upon fact means that one cannot find a secure, unchanging order beneath history—we only know the order we find, and that order does not precede history. Rather, it proceeds from history, that is, from concrete relations. We are not able to find underneath or beyond historical experience some primal order that is not itself historicized. Jacques Derrida has rebelled against the orderly interpretation of experience in the sense of a *logos* that is internal to reality. He calls for the deconstruction of that order, and stresses the character of history as serial interpretations. Dean summarizes the implications of Derrida's deconstructionist thought as follows:

> The deconstructionist and the American religious empiricist both recognize that God is continually reinterpreted in history. However, a deconstructionist historical method specifies the historical meaning of theological terms, and the ways in which that historical meaning is comprised of a chain of reinterpretations.[47]

Let us see how that sense of historical unfolding as a series of reinterpretations of reinterpretations can play itself out in the case of Jesus and subsequent Christian history.

Jesus' experience of God is interpreted already in the process of his experiencing God as a Jew (a Buddhist *could not* have had Jesus' experience of God). That interpreted experience of Jesus is the revelational event in which Christian existence is grounded. When Jesus, after the fact of his own experience, articulates it in turn to his companions, he further interprets it: he says who God is, and what difference the "who" of God makes for how all of us are called to be together in this world (the reign of God). Those who later preached Jesus' teaching further reinterpreted it so that it could be understood by people in Antioch, Athens, and Rome. Each later interpretation always worms its way into the content of the "fact" of Jesus' experience.

Not only do individuals interpret. Interpretation is also a social function of communities. The Christian scriptures are written records of the normative interpretations of various Christian communities. They reflect the social situations of these communities.[48] The Gospel writer (or Letter writer) speaks for and to a community, and in so doing, he himself interprets further the community interpretation. Our scriptures are not the primordial revelational event. They are a witness to the event. Their canonization is the larger community's validation of their trustworthiness in transmitting the power of the original revelation. Canonization also implies that historical interpretation is a continuation of the revelation.

Christianity's originating revelational event is the life of Jesus, a Galilean Jew from the early first century CE. Interpretation began immediately. In the second volume I will indicate that in the Christian scriptures themselves there are three and a half root metaphors, each of which has the power to generate a Christian story, though in fact only one of them substantially did so in Western Christianity.

In the third volume I am interested in retrieving one of the metaphors (actually an interrelated duo of metaphors) that did not spin out a major christological belief system. This earliest of the root metaphors is more indigenously Jewish and is clearly part of the religious world of Jesus himself (it focuses upon the Spirit of God and the Word of God). The second metaphor is the Wisdom figure, which syncretistically is about middle way between Jewish and Greek instincts. The Wisdom figure probably did not play into Jesus' own sense of God. The third metaphor is the *Logos*/Word understanding of God, which shows up in two forms in Christian scriptures. We find *logos* used in the Letter to the Hebrews in a way that is quite of a piece with Philo's interpretation of *logos*. There is a somewhat similar use of *logos* in John's Gospel, yet with a very important difference. Thus I count *logos* as a metaphor and a half. Almost certainly, *logos* does not play into Jesus' experience of God; it is not part of his religious culture and therefore can not help interpret and construct his experience of God.

My concern in this project is to call the first of these metaphors, the *Ruach/Dabhar* combination, into a kind of serious conversation in which it has not yet sufficiently engaged. The Jewishness of Jesus requires that this conversation get under way at long last.

Conversation

Gadamer has recommended the image of "conversation" for clarifying how the interpretation of experience (of texts, of people, of events) brings us to understanding. Conversation, in the richer senses of the word, is not just one of the things two people do. Conversation concretely constructs the relationship, and in so doing builds the identity of both parties. I want to compare the function of conversation in building a relationship with the notion of theology as conversation.

A relationship. Two people meet for the first time. Each presumes some things about the other. Each immediately and instinctively makes some initial judgments about the other. We are usually able to have some initial understandings because we live in the same world and have gone through some of the same events of history. While it is true that we begin with some shared world, it is also true that each of us enters into the new meeting with a lot of "old history" that we don't share. We rarely recognize how much our unshared old history also generates some understandings out of which we form our first appraisals (initial understandings) of each other. We can never become fully aware of all the presuppositions that lead us to the judgments we make, but whatever can be brought to awareness will help the conversation.

Now to theology. When we in the late twentieth century meet the Jesus-event and engage it in conversation, we of course bring our twentieth century pre-understandings with us. And, as David Tracy says, "what contemporary theologians do attempt, under the rubric of interpretation of our cultural situation, is to render that preunderstanding as explicit as possible."[49] When we explore the Jewish world of Jesus, for example, it is important to remember that our psychological understandings of personality and subjectivity differ, not totally, perhaps, but significantly with Jesus' or Paul's understandings of human existence. But to hear Jesus, we must grant him his meanings as fully as we can manage. Knowing our own meanings is a necessary early step.

Back to relationship. Because of mutual attraction, we two begin to talk. In all our talking we disclose little things about ourselves. We receive new information about the other. If the sharing continues, each of us soon becomes aware of the otherness of the other. We recognize things about the other that are not easy to understand. We experience distance and remoteness, and our ability to listen well is genuinely taxed. If the relationship is to grow in healthy ways, I must struggle to break out of my own prejudices (pre-understandings), and try to listen as neutrally as possible to the other life as it tells itself on its own grounds. I can only genuinely hear another life if I grant the other his/her own ground as my basis for interpreting what is said or meant—even if I do not agree. Granting the other his/her own ground is a move that begins to overcome some of the remoteness, but no one can ever overcome all of the otherness of an other.

To theology. The need for interpretation is consciously recognized when the experience of otherness is clear, when we are aware of the distance between us now and the fact or text being interpreted. "Interpretation, philosophically understood, is nothing more than an attempt to make estrangement and distinction productive."[50] As in true conversation, so in theology, I accept the otherness as worthy of consideration, and try to get inside it to such an extent as to understand not just the particular issue, but the larger framework out of which it is said.[51]

Historical biblical criticism has over and over made us aware of how different are the worlds of meaning that constituted first century Palestinian Judaism. There is estrangement to be broached. When we have repeatedly been caught up short by discovering that what we thought we knew is actually not quite the case at all, we can learn what Gadamer calls a "trained receptivity" to the otherness of a past event. For me, repeated confrontation with the Jewishness of Jesus has asked for trained receptivity to otherness at many turns of the road, especially in conversation on that less travelled Galilean road.

To relationship. The otherness I encounter raises a question in my mind.

If I choose to remain in the new relationship, I stay with the conversation until some answer comes back to me. The otherness that my counterpart experiences in me initiates the same question and answer pattern. Because two people are different from the start, and because two people continue to have different experiences as a relationship builds, the to and fro movement of question and answer is a "fundamental procedure" to "the living presence of conversation."[52]

To theology. Gadamer adds that the to and fro movement of true conversation has some of the characteristics of a game that is played. In tennis or in football, for example, experienced players who know the game rules get engrossed in the game, without much consciousness about the rules to be followed. One just plays the game heart and soul. Or better yet, at such a point the game plays us heart and soul. In this context, the incessant movements of interpretation and understanding are quite like a game—not one game among many, but precisely the game of being human. Conversation is the substance of commitment to a living relationship with a sacred text, or with a tradition.

To relationship. Conversation is not just verbal talk between people. It is the continuing to and fro movement, the relentless cycle of questions and answers. It is the risk-taking that daily characterizes the game of life. Conversation is an image for the relational dynamics that are the relationship. As we converse, we build the selves that meet each other. Conversing keeps construction underway, and new construction requires ongoing conversation. That constant cycle IS the relationship, full of risk, change, pain, satisfaction, movement, challenge, and reward.

To theology. Christian life is constituted by its conversation with the Jesus-event and with history that the Jesus-event has subsequently made. The christology of any period is the shape of the conversation at that moment. The history of theology is eavesdropping on the conversations of the ages. That characterization alone is not fully adequate, but it is fully accurate.

No less than people in relationship, the church finds itself engaged in a to and fro movement of question and answer with its most basic texts of scripture and tradition. It is becoming more aware of distantness and otherness, and the necessity of interpretation to understand its own past. Time-boundedness relativizes, of course. However, it doesn't relativize normativeness out of existence, but struggles to relocate it in the trustworthiness of time-bound talk rather than in the stable content of timeless talk.

To relationship. The honest attempt to grant another person his/her own grounds is full of risk. The honesty of this attempt means suspending judgment in order to listen. It means relinquishing the familiar and entering into an alien land. It means that I shall surely be shaped by the otherness I experience there.

Once I have been receptive to otherness, I can never come home the same. That is the risk: I never know ahead of time what kind of self I'll bring back home. I am *always* different after taking in otherness. Even if I don't agree, my horizon has been altered, and my world is larger and more variegated. It is a risk.

It would be hard to overestimate the importance of letting another voice speak from its own horizon as much as we are able. Granted, we can never stand within another's horizon in the same way as the one for whom the horizon is indigenous. The otherness of another's world may be small or may be large. But it is a safe presumption that otherness always exists, and that I must work very hard indeed to hear the other voice on its own ground.

To theology. Since the rise of historical consciousness, doing theology has been experienced as riskier than in times past. The perceived (in earlier times) timelessness of normative pronouncements has been historicized. We recognize how often scriptural texts have been read in the light of dogma, and were not heard in their original voice. In the synoptic Gospels, ''Son of Man'' often designates the other worldly figure who comes upon clouds at the end of the world; and ''Son of God'' designates a human being chosen by God to do God's work in human history. However, read in the light of Chalcedon's two-nature christology, those meanings were often reversed so that Son of Man named the humanity and Son of God named the divinity of Jesus. No small part of the church's present agenda is to affirm and explicate the necessary functions of normativeness in a Christian community, but to do so in a fully time-bound way.

When the church hears its scriptures or tradition with fresh ears, that is, when with the tools of historical criticism it hears something different than it heard before, it finds some of its being put indeed at risk.[53] I think, for example, of the very different historical reading of Christian origins that Elisabeth Schüssler-Fiorenza presents.[54] It is an institutional surprise to retrieve the splendid contributions of women to the formation of the early church. These are ''dangerous memories'' because they put present patriarchal practices under suspicion. These are institutionally painful moments of ecclesial conversation, because hearing something new *makes* something new, and it hurts to get remade.

To hear Jesus speak to us with the full weight of his Jewishness behind his words is to hear about Christian origins with fresh ears. There is no way that this conversation cannot put some precious historical perceptions at risk.

To relationship. I always enter a relationship from the perspective of my world. When I meet someone, I view him/her on my horizons, but I am encountering someone with a different world who experiences on a different horizon. I open myself to the otherness, and try to understand from that different horizon. If we genuinely meet there has been some fusion of horizons. Gadamer reminds us that fusion of horizons never means two contrasting horizons have been simply and totally fused. There is always some tension between one and another that is not resolved in the partial fusion of horizons. No "other" person or "other" event can be rescued from its otherness without remainder. I should never say that "I know *exactly* what you mean." Keeping the tension exposed is part of the hermeneutic task.[55]

To theology. There is much about the Jewish horizon of Jesus that can be retrieved. I would not be writing this book if I did not think so. Nor would I be writing this book if I didn't think the retrieving conversation had a strong and lovely world out in front of it. However, I acknowledge the inevitability of tension between a twentieth century interpretation of that Jewishness and the aromas of kosher cooking pushed out onto the streets of Capernaum by the lake breezes of Galilee in Jesus' day.

To relationship. We reckon daily, and sometimes minute by minute, with the undecidedness of the future. The texture of a relationship at any given moment influences greatly what kinds of possible relational worlds stand out there in front of two people. The worlds out in front of them are part and parcel of the very meaning of their relationship. New conversation always gets new possibility projected out there in front. No matter how much people think they know about how their life together will look, I think no married couple will ever say at any time, "this is *exactly* how we knew it would turn out." The world out in front of friends or spouses is built and rebuilt and re-rebuilt out of the interpreting conversations that *are* their life together.

To theology. Martin Heidegger's work is in many ways seminal to the hermeneutical tradition. He insists that it is the function of understanding "to . . . always press forward into possibilities. . . . Understanding has itself the existential structure which we call '*projection.*' "[56] Making a possible world stand up out in front of conversants—this is what every act of interpretation does.

Interpretation is not only a reflection of an experience, it actually constructs experience. Gadamer takes up Hegel's sense that the human spirit is engaged in the *building (Bildung)* of human culture.[57] We are accustomed to think that scientific knowledge, for example, is our mirroring of what nature has already made. Rorty reminds us that science itself doesn't just mirror: *it makes.*[58]

Theology likewise is not an organized, mirror-like understanding of the faith that has been given us. Theology does, of course, spring out of a history which it seeks to interpret, but the interpreting *makes* a particular kind of Christian world stand up out there in front of the faithful community. We have a better sense now, for example, that Augustinian Platonism helped make a world ahead of it, and so did Aristotelian Thomism. All Western Christian lives today stand in front of Augustine and Thomas. Subtract those theologies/ conversations from Christian history and it would be a far different story that we tell with our Christian lives today.

A theological conversation between the Jewishness of Jesus and our own age makes a different world of Christian possibility present itself out there in front of us. The differences are sometimes in the shape of new things that turn up, and sometimes in the shape of accustomed things that do not. The differences are in mood and mode of relationship with God. This present work is just a tiny little moment of early morning Christian conversation with an all but abandoned horizon for the Christian fact.

Reprise

Although I am not particularly fond of the name "process theology," I have moved in that tradition for some two decades now. I continue to be fascinated by and convinced about Whitehead's large vision of the primacy of becoming and the ultimacy of relatedness. About some of the technical details I am less satisfied. Increasingly, however, the empirical side of this tradition seems to me its best gift to theology: in our claims we must never transgress beyond what lived experience provokes.[59] That includes, of course, the "imaginative" aspect of generalization upon experience. But the imagination is still in the direction of and at the invitation of experience.

The pragmatic/empirical tradition is surely among our better articulations of the indigenous American spirit, as pluralistic as that spirit is. As James noted, religious experience seems to feel that empiricism is hostile, while all the time it could really be a best friend. I hope that best friend status is soon conferred!

The empirical approach that I have described in this opening chapter combines several traditions that are quite congenial to one another:

—empiricism in the Jamesian and Whiteheadian senses, as further elaborated by William Dean and others to attend diligently to its historicist temper;

—the metaphorical tradition that insists upon the imaged and analogical ways we perceive, feel, know and communicate;

—and the hermeneutical tradition that recommends highly disciplined conversation as an image not only of interpreted experience, but of world-making.

To interpret another voice accurately requires that we let it speak out of its own world. For historical reasons that are not hard to indicate, the voice of Jesus has rarely spoken to his followers across the centuries out of his own thoroughgoing Jewishness. I will be trying to understand the Judaism of Galilean Palestine in the time of Jesus. That does not, of course, give us immediate access to his subjectivity. But if we understand the religious and cultural matrix in which his human consciousness awakened, we know something real about his subjectivity. My intentions for Chapter Two are to explore a very complex question: How indigenously Jewish and how Hellenized was Galilean Judaism in Jesus' time, and what is likely to have been his assumptive world? We want to understand better the cultural world of Jesus so that we can hear him speak with his ownmost voice.

Chapter Three continues the discussion of Chapter Two, but from a different perspective. We will look at several "types" of Jews that have been used to help locate Jesus within his Jewishness. We will look at Jesus' relationship with the Pharisees. We will view him as a teacher, and as a wandering charismatic preacher. And finally we will examine the figure of the eschatological prophet.

This first volume is committed to getting our conversation started on the less travelled road.

The second volume will address three and a half root metaphors about who God is and how God is present among us. These are all root metaphors that have been pressed into service to interpret the meaning of Jesus. Only one of these three (the *Ruach*/Spirit of God working hand in hand with the *Dabhar*/Word of God) seems likely to have been part of Jesus' own assumptive world. With that metaphor we shall converse at length in the final volume.

The third volume is committed to asking what kind of world is made to stand up out there in front of us in these latter decades of the second millennium, as a result of our sustained conversation on the less travelled road. It is not an idle question. I stand among those who suspect that something serious has gone wrong with the directions in which Western history has been moving. I do not mean a few problematic areas. I mean central aspects of the fundamental Western social construction of reality. I also stand among those who believe that in the deep story of the Good News of Jesus Christ there is an engaging alternative to self-destruction. And I am fully convinced that reconnecting with Christianity's own essential, but long repudiated, Jewishness will help us redeem our waywardness, as well as help us recognize those forms of our togetherness that are not wayward but right, i.e., the wonders of our relational experience that require jubilees to celebrate them.

Notes

1. William James, *Essays in Radical Empiricism* and *A Pluralistic Universe* (Gloucester: Peter Smith, 1967).

2. Alfred North Whitehead, *Process and Reality,* corrected edition (New York: Freepress, 1978), pp. 3–17.

3. William Dean, *American Religious Empiricism* (Albany: SUNY, 1986), esp. chapter 2.

4. Whitehead, 1978, p. 4.

5. Paul Ricoeur, *The Symbolism of Evil* (Boston: Beacon, 1979), "The Symbol Gives Rise to Thought," pp. 347–357.

6. Hans-Georg Gadamer, *Truth and Method* (New York: Crossroad, 1975), e.g., pp. 330ff.

7. Richard Rorty, *Philosophy and the Mirror of Nature* (Princeton: Princeton Univ. Press, 1979), esp. part III.

8. Nelson Goodman, *Ways of Worldmaking* (Indianapolis: Hackett, 1978).

9. Robert M. Grant with David Tracy, *A Short History of the Interpretation of the Bible* (Philadelphia: Fortress, 1984), chapters 16–18.

10. William James, RE 1967, pp. 314–315.

11. Dean, 1986, p. 38.

12. Dean, 1986, pp. 20–21.

13. Dean, 1986, p. 6.

14. Whitehead, 1978, p. 200.

15. Alfred North Whitehead, *Modes of Thought* (New York: Capricorn, 1958), p. 188.

16. Alan Watts, *The Book* (New York: Vintage, 1972), p. 87.

17. Bernard E. Meland, *Higher Education and the Human Spirit* (Chicago: Univ. of Chicago Press, 1953), p. 62.

18. Michael Wyschogrod, *The Body of Faith: Judaism as Corporeal Election* (New York: Seabury, 1983), p. 9.

19. Wyschogrod, 1983, pp. 15–26.

20. Bernard E. Meland, *Faith and Culture* (Carbondale: Univ. of So. Illinois, 1972), p. 35.

21. James, RE 1967, p. 321.

22. Alfred North Whitehead, *Adventures of Ideas* (New York: Freepress, 1967), p. 270.

23. Martin Heidegger, *Being and Time* (London: SCM, 1962), p. 43.

24. Bernard E. Meland, *Fallible Forms and Symbols* (Philadelphia: Fortress, 1976), p. 148.

25. Peter Berger, *A Rumor of Angels* (Garden City: Doubleday, 1970), chapter 2; and *The Heretical Imperative* (Garden City: Doubleday, 1979), esp. chapter 5.

26. Piet Schoonenberg, "Trinity: The Consummated Covenant—Theses on the Doctrine of the Trinity," *Science Religieuse/Studies in Religion*, Fall 1975, p. 111.

27. Whitehead, 1978, p. 13.

28. Whitehead, 1978, p. 5.

29. James, 1967, p. 42.

30. Watts, 1972, p. 8.

31. Whitehead, 1978, p. 13.

32. Alfred North Whitehead, *The Function of Reason* (Boston: Beacon, 1962), p. 82.

33. Whitehead, 1962, p. 82.

34. Charles Sanders Peirce, Justus Buchler, ed., *Philosophical Writings of Peirce* (New York: Dover, 1965), p. 30.

35. William James, *Pragmatism* (New York: Washington Square, 1963), p. 25.

36. James, 1963, p. 25.

37. Sally McFague, *Metaphorical Theology* (Philadelphia: Fortress, 1982), p. 15.

38. Paul Ricoeur, *The Rule of Metaphor* (Toronto: Univ. of Toronto, 1979), p. 63.

39. McFague, 1982, p. 13.

40. Ricoeur, 1979, pp. 248–249.

41. Ricoeur, 1979, p. 249.

42. Ricoeur, 1979, p. 244.

43. Gadamer, 1975, pp. 415–416.

44. Milan Kundera, *The Unbearable Lightness of Being* (New York: Harper, 1984), pp. 10–11.

45. Kundera, 1984, p. 221.

46. Dean, 1986, p. 221.

47. Dean, 1986, p. 56.

48. Cf. Raymond E. Brown, *The Churches the Apostles Left Behind* (New York: Paulist, 1984).

49. Grant/Tracy, 1984, p. 172.

50. Paul Ricoeur, *Interpretation* (Ft. Worth: Texas Christian Univ., 1976), p. 44.

51. Gadamer, 1975, p. 347.

52. Gadamer, 1975, p. 331.

53. For a fuller discussion of how a community's conversation with scripture puts its status quo at risk, see my chapter in, Bernard J. Lee, ed., *Eucharist* (Collegeville: The Liturgical Press, 1987), "Shared Homily: Conversation That Puts Communities at Risk," pp. 157–174.

54. Elisabeth Schüssler-Fiorenza, *In Memory of Her* (New York: Crossroad, 1983).

55. Gadamer, 1975, p. 273.

56. Heidegger, 1962, pp. 184–185.

57. Gadamer, 1975, pp. 10–19.

58. Rorty, 1979, p. 344.

59. Bernard J. Lee, "Two Process Theologies," *Theological Studies* 45 (1984), pp. 307–319.

2
Galilean Jewishness

Christianity arose on Jewish soil; Jesus and the Apostles spoke Aramaic. . . . As the New Testament writings show, they were firmly rooted in the Old Testament and lived in its world of images. Shortly after the death of the Founder, however, the new religious community's center of gravity shifted to the Greek-speaking Hellenistic world, and after the year 70, the community was severed finally from its motherland: Christianity has been the religion of Europe ever since. It is significant, however, that despite their absolute authority the words of Jesus were preserved by the Church only in the Greek language. Not only are these two languages essentially different, but so too are the kinds of images and thinking involved in them. This distinction goes very deeply into the psychic life; the Jews themselves defined their spiritual predisposition as anti-Hellenic. Once this point is properly understood, it must be granted completely.

Thorlief Boman[1]

Retrieving Galilean Jewishness

In a true conversation, each person struggles to hear the other on the other's own ground. Every voice is thick with history, both personal and cultural. Every listener's ears are just as thick with history. The recovery of a voice from long ago is never simple and never total. As the opening text of this chapter suggests, very much of the Jewish voice of Jesus that spoke in Aramaic has been transmitted as heard by Greek ears and in the Greek language.

From the late eighteenth century into the early twentieth century, the desire to recover the historical voice of Jesus was carried on as the "quest of the historical Jesus."[2] We have learned since then some wrong ways, some ineffective ways, and also some helpful ways to try to allow this voice to speak *on its own* in true conversation.[3] We look not so much for the authentic words of Jesus as the authentic voice of Jesus. Because our earliest texts are Greek, we are not certain about the original words in any single thing that Jesus said, with the possible exception of an occasional phrase actually transmitted in Aramaic, such as *Abba* (the intimate form of "Father"); *Talitha Kum* ("Little girl, arise!"); and *Eloi, Eloi, lama sabachthani* ("My God, my God, why have you forsaken me"). That is not thick enough history to recover the full throated voice of Jesus. The early quest for the historical Jesus indicated the futility of seeking the original words, the *verba ipsissima* of Jesus.

MAP

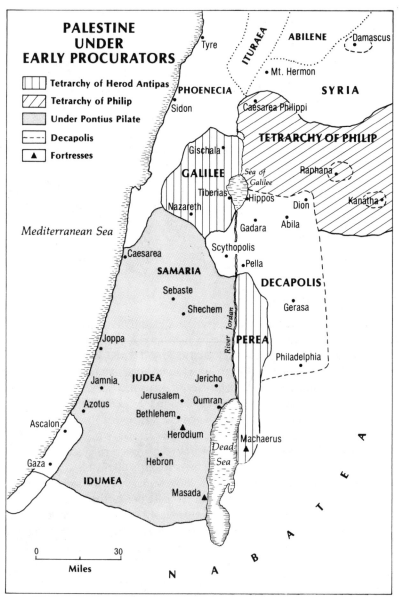

**PALESTINE
UNDER
EARLY PROCURATORS**

	Tetrarchy of Herod Antipas
	Tetrarchy of Philip
	Under Pontius Pilate
- - -	Decapolis
▲	Fortresses

ITURAEA

ABILENE

Damascus

Tyre

PHOENECIA

Sidon

Mt. Hermon

SYRIA

Caesarea Philippi

Gischala

GALILEE

Sea of Galilee

TETRARCHY OF PHILIP

Raphana

Tiberias

Hippos

Dion

Kanatha

Nazareth

Mediterranean Sea

Gadara

Abila

Scythopolis

Caesarea

Pella

SAMARIA

DECAPOLIS

Sebaste

Shechem

Gerasa

River Jordan

PEREA

Joppa

Jamnia

JUDEA

Jericho

Philadelphia

Azotus

Jerusalem

Qumran

Ascalon

Bethlehem

Herodium

Machaerus

Gaza

Dead Sea

Hebron

IDUMEA

Masada

0   30

Miles

N   A   B   A   T   E   A

54

A "new quest" was undertaken a half century later, with a certain security that at least the basic message, the *kerygma,* could be recovered as authentic teaching of Jesus, the *vox ipsissima.*[4] Through form criticism and editorial criticism some of the interpretive layers can be identified. The sacred text, submitted to historical criticism, is still not transparent to the historical figure of Jesus, but it is at least translucent: some light pierces through. The hermeneutical tradition has further deepened our appropriation of Jesus' teaching, by locating meaning out in front of the text as well as in the socio-historical setting behind the text.

My concerns in this book are allied to those of the historical quest—but not identical. I am concerned to establish some sense of the Jewishness of Jesus by exploring the historical, cultural and social setting of Galilee. One major concern is how much Greekness has impinged upon the Jewishness of the cultural milieu in which the consciousness of Jesus was incubated. The influence of Greek culture upon most of the Mediterranean world was significant, and that includes Palestinian Judaism. However, the influence of Greek culture upon Judaism was different in Alexandria than in Rome, different in Athens than in Palestine, and (I want to hold) different even in Galilean Palestine than in Judean Palestine. While we cannot enter into the subjectivity of Jesus, if we can ascertain with some security, as I think we can, what his assumptive world was like, we stand a better chance of authentically hearing the basic proclamation of the Good News. By "assumptive world" I include the formative emotions of Judaism (as Jacob Neusner calls them) as well as the formative ideas.

My serious interest and my curiosity led me, as they have led other Christians, to the places where Jesus lived. One morning, as I wandered slowly through the streets of Capernaum, which was the center of much of Jesus' activity, I found myself wondering what his life had been like before his sudden appearance in the Gospels as an adult. I know that no one ever suddenly appears on the public scene with the kind of presence we encounter in Jesus. One doesn't begin that way. People who are effective presences anywhere are schooled by historical experience and instructed well by their socio-historical circumstances. They have been challenged by their relationships, pressured and summoned by events, and have made imaginative, perceptive, and sometimes original choices in response to all of that. Events, relations and choices coalesce. Out of that coalescence identity emerges. How and where did Jesus get practiced enough, his sensibilities finely hewn enough, that his life made both Jewish and Roman ears perk up and sent tremors through their bodies politic?

Historical recollections in the Later Scriptures suggest that even Jesus' peers raised similar questions. "This is the carpenter's son, surely? Is not his mother the woman called Mary, and his brothers James and Joseph and Simon and Jude? His sisters, too, are they not all here with us? So where did the man get it all?" (Mt 13:55). He was a puzzle even for his family. He returned home to Capernaum, "and once more such a crowd collected that they could not even have a meal. When his relatives heard of this, they set out to take charge of him; they said, 'He is out of his mind' " (Mk 3:20–21). A few verses later Mark indicates that the relatives are Jesus' mother and his brothers.

Those questions haunted me as well as I walked through unearthed streets, houses, shops and the synagogue of Capernaum. Jesus spent most of his adult life there. Why did he leave Nazareth and move to Capernaum? What kinds of intrigue got perpetrated in the shadowy nooks of this Galilean fishing village? Who were his close friends, who his mentors?

Practically, no concrete information about such matters is to be had. I presume with most historical-critical exegesis that the first historical/biographical information we have about Jesus is his baptism by John. But there is information of a more general kind about which it is both legitimate and fruitful to inquire. All children of all ages are profoundly and permanently shaped by the socio-cultural world in which mind and heart awaken to consciousness. There are resources to help us reconstruct with reasonable accuracy the cultural and religious milieu which was the world to which Jesus awoke. There is help from ancient texts and from critical interpretation of them, from archaeology, from both Jewish and Christian historical studies, and from the use of sociological paradigms to help interpret events and personalities. Taken together, I am confident that we can assemble a bold-stroked picture of critical parts of the relational web in whose womb the identity of Jesus was nurtured. Putting that picture together is part of conversation's task in allowing a voice to speak from its own world.

To converse securely with the Jesus-event, we have to take seriously the utter Jewishness of Jesus. It is a Galilean Jewishness. Whatever it is that Jesus is up to, it is as a Jew *within his particular world of Judaism*. His sense of himself, his vocation, his destiny, even his identity, all exist without remainder within the ferment of his Jewish understandings of God and world and history—what Buber has called the impulses and emotions of his essential Jewishness.

Although it is clear that Christianity is founded in Jesus Christ, it seems most unlikely, as I have already indicated, that Jesus intended to found a new form of institutionalized religion. The institutional forms of Christianity that differentiate it from Judaism are historical emergents responding to historical circumstances. Earliest Christian self-understanding presumes that the followers of Jesus are a movement *within* Judaism, one which Christians perceive to bring fulfillment to the inheritance, but not to initiate a new and separate historical trajectory. A creative transformation of the inherited Covenant is entirely consonant with Jewish history. The Covenant had already undergone successive transformations. Only when this connectedness of Jesus and of our origins to Judaism is fully appreciated can we begin adequately to understand what has emerged as a distinctive Christian structure of experience.

It is not my intention to construe the christological meaning of Jesus so Hebraically that everything is religiously smooth and debateless between us Christians and our Jewish sisters and brothers. We have too much complex historical experience for that. My hope is that we Christians might find some effective ways to reappropriate the Jewishness of *our own* inheritance. I perceive power there that we have too long been without. I, along with others who work at the retrieval of the Jewishness of Jesus, need the on-going critical reaction of our Jewish brothers and sisters. When we Christians try to tell the story of Jewishness, we must be assured that Jews recognize it as their story (or one of their stories).

Even so, I want to acknowledge that even with re-won affection for our own Semitic moorings, we Christians cannot ever erase the horrors of past history in which our antisemitism has formidable complicity. But we can give new history a different face. We Christians can entertain some new tendernesses for the continuing strong presence in history of all the children of Israel. Their God and our God is one God: the Father of Abraham, Isaac, Jacob, Ruth, Susanna, Jesus, Mary, Martha, Peter, John, etc.

I am interested in the fuller christological recovery of the Jewishness of Jesus for a number of reasons. The first is a matter of historical accuracy: that Jesus was a faithful, religious Jew. We Christians cannot understand ourselves accurately if our self-interpretation is fundamentally at odds with the truth of our beginnings. The fact is that our christologies have often been at odds with the truth of our beginnings, notably in their supersessionist features.

Second, because our world so desperately needs religious conviction that can provide a basis for world community, it becomes vital that theology be done in dialogue with other great religious traditions of the world. Instead of asserting our universal claims against each other, we should receive each other's experience with a willingness to be shaped by what we find there in each other's otherness. In a word, the cry of our age is for a final detribalization of deity. The openness of the major religious traditions of the world to each other's experience is absolutely requisite for such detribalization. For Christians, no partner in dialogic community is as necessary as Judaism.

Third, process/relational modes of thought, especially in their

Whiteheadian version, are a contemporary world view much more congenial to Hebrew thought than is the Greek mind. Thus, the recovery of the Jewishness of Jesus with the assistance of a process/relational hermeneutic might help re-expose the Christ-event to Western Christianity for some new modes of appropriation. This is an effort that weaves in and out of all three volumes. In my use of process/relational modes of thought, I am not as much concerned with the categorcial details of process thought as for their general import (the ultimacy of becoming and the primacy of relationships) and for their empirical steadfastness. Only at the end of the third volume will I address a few quite specific issues in direct conversation with Whitehead's systematic philosophy.

The fourth reason why I am personally interested in and committed to a Christian recovery of our own Jewishness is for the sake of the Christian story. The recovery of this Jewishness suggests some quite new ways in which Christian existence might be construed. We begin to feel that something else might be the case than is the case, and that it could be something true and beautiful. I am convinced that the retrieval of Jesus' Jewishness offers some strong new ways in which the Christian Good News can accost experience today.

In this chapter I will be concerned about the general character of Galilee in Jesus' time. Galilee, of course, shares much with the rest of Palestinian Judaism. But it is also conditioned by a different geography and some different history than the Judaism of the south. It has its own religious texture, its own ethos, its own political mood. The better we know these things, the easier it becomes to hear the voice of Jesus speaking out of its own world.

How Hellenized was Galilee, and in what ways? That is a singularly touchy question. The kinds of resources that would provide an undisputably clear answer do not exist, and the best scholars on the question are not in secure agreement about how to interpret the evidence that does exist. I will indicate my judgment on the matter. As the chapter unfolds, I will also indicate why the question is so important in the first place. The surface way of asking the questions is: how much Greek did educated Galileans speak or read or write? The deeper question is: what worlds of meaning did the consciousness of Jesus and his early followers inhabit?

Galilee: Some Geography and History

The ancient land of Canaan was important to the Hebrews because it became a Land of Promise essentially related to their Covenant with Yahweh. This tiny area on the Mediterranean coast has few natural resources. Except for a small area in the Galilee region, its readily tillable land is meager. Palestine, however, is a critical piece of land for other reasons. It is where three continents meet: Europe, Asia and Africa. Conquering armies came from each of these continents and ruled Palestine at different times: Babylonians and Syrians from Asia, Egyptians from Africa, Greeks and Romans from Europe. It is where the civilization of the West encounters that of the East. It is where the cultures and temperaments of the South meet those of the North.

I am particularly interested in the question of cultural traditions that shaped Palestinian and specifically Galilean Judaism in the time of Jesus, especially the relation between Greek and more indigenously Hebraic culture. There are excellent studies of the relation between Judaism and Hellenism by both Jewish[5] and Christian[6] scholars. All are agreed that by the first centuries BCE and CE no part of Judaism was untouched by Hellenism. But not all parts were touched in the same way or to the same extent. For example, the book of Qoheleth which reflects Judaism in Jerusalem, around 150 BCE, is clearly marked by Greek influence. However, the Greek mind does not make its way into the internal workings of the Jewish mind of Qoheleth, as it does in the case of Philo of Alexandria, whose life overlapped the life of Jesus.

Tracing historical events in this chapter is a necessary part of our attempt to hear Jesus in his own voice. Archeologists have uncovered Greek pottery in Palestine from the sixth century BCE in various sites along the coastline.[7] However, the major contact between Greek and Jewish culture follows upon the expeditions of Alexander the Great in 331–321 BCE. At this time, Alexander wrests control of Palestine from the Persian, Darius. When Alexander dies in 321, his generals lodge conflicting claims to Palestinian territory which is caught between the Seleucids to the northeast (Syria) and the Ptolemies to the southwest (Egypt). We must consider a century of rule under the Ptolemies (from Egypt), 301–201 BCE; then a very different period of rule under the Seleucids from 201 until the success of the Hasmonean revolution; and finally the Roman rule beginning with Pompey's conquests, c. 65 BCE.

My concern is with what is happening to Jewish religion and culture as Palestinian life encounters these other cultural systems in significant ways. Of special interest for the purposes of this work is the Palestinian Jewishness of Galilee, in the northern part of the country. And even here, one must note the difference between upper and lower Galilee. It is the latter which is the context for Jesus. For the particular focus upon Galilean Judaism I am especially indebted to the work of Geza Vermès[8] and to Sean Freyne's detailed, extensive and careful study of Galilee.[9] These two do not treat all the same issues, and sometimes they do not agree about the same issues (though often they do). But together they help draw a reliable picture of the Galilean Judaism in which Jesus lived.

The ancient land of the Hebrews stretches about eighty-five miles from

Bersheva south in the Negev desert to Dan in the north above the Sea of Galilee. From the Mediterranean coast to the Jordan river at the level of Jerusalem in the south is about thirty miles. From the coast to the Sea of Galilee in the north, at the level of Capernaum, is only about twenty miles. In earlier history, Galilee was in the northern Kingdom of Israel, Jerusalem in the southern Kingdom of Judea. In the first century CE Judea is still the name for the lower part of Palestine (the name "Palestine" is probably a corruption of "Philistine"). Judea is centered on Jerusalem. Just north of Judea is Samaria, a Semitic people angrily estranged from the other Jews of Palestine at the time. The Samaritans refuse the Oral Tradition of the Torah and reject the Temple at Jerusalem. The antagonism between the Samaritans and the Jews is bitter and often dangerous. Galilee is north, just above Samaria, and is therefore significantly separated from Judea by the hostile Samaritan territory. It is divided into Upper and Lower Galilee. Terrain and climate as well as commercial orientation mark the difference. Josephus says that Upper Galilee begins where the sycamore trees no longer grow (roughly a line from the top of the Sea of Galilee west to the coast). The mountains are higher, rain more plentiful, land more fertile. Commercially, Upper Galilee is oriented toward the seaports of Tyre and Sidon (in current Lebanon), Lower Galilee toward the port at Ptolemais (present day Haifa).

In the Gospels Jesus is regularly enough identified with Nazareth that we may presume he was in fact raised there. The village of Nazareth is in the center of Lower Galilee. Most of Jesus' public life centers around three towns whose orientation is to the fishing industry of the Sea of Galilee with some agriculture as well: Capernaum, Bethsaida and Chorozain. Lower Galilee, then, is our primary interest in this immediate consideration.

To establish a Greek city, a *polis,* in a conquered land is the Greek way of Hellenizing the region. The city of Alexandria on the north African coast is a classic and effective example. During the century in which Palestine is under the Ptolemies (301–201 BCE) no attempt is made to establish a Greek *polis* in any part of Palestine. The port city of Ptolemais is not a new city, only one whose facilities are improved, with the name of the Ptolemies given it (previously it was called Accho). The Ptolemies, and in this they contrast significantly with the Seleucids who follow them, do not attempt to inculturate the area to Hellenistic mores or language.[10]

The political sway of the Ptolemies begins to loosen in 221 BCE when the Syrian King Antiochus III attacks northern Galilee. In 201 BCE he takes control of Palestine from the Ptolemies with only minimal opposition. The rule of Antiochus IV Epiphanes from 175–163 BCE marks a very crucial period for the history of Judaism. The Pharisees emerge during these and subsequent years with immense power and with an Oral Tradition that marks a significant evolution in religious belief, practice and structures. I will address these issues in a more sustained way in the following chapter, because of the vital importance of the Pharisees to the Judaism of the time of Jesus. What precipitates the great crisis of this period is the forced Hellenization which Epiphanes organizes in collaboration with some Hellenizing Jews in Palestine. In 167 BCE, Epiphanes converts the Temple in Jerusalem into a shrine to Zeus and forbids the practice of circumcision.

The Maccabean revolt ends the Seleucid rule. Various family members of the Hasmonean house, the Maccabees, lead Jewish resistance to this forced Hellenization and desecration. In 164 BCE the Temple is retaken and rededicated (which the feast of Hanukkah continues to celebrate in our era). The Maccabees succeed militarily in retaking much of what had earlier been the kingdoms of Israel and Judea, and establish once again a Jewish kingdom. Politically, the Hasmonean dynasty restores a Kingdom to the Jews and thus returns to them control over their lives and destiny.

Religiously, however, the solution is not without an edge: the Hasmonean dynasty is not a Davidic dynasty, which is where the messianic promise lies; and the high priesthood becomes a political appointment rather than a position reserved for a Zadokite, according to biblical directives. These two factors help make Pharisaic support of the Hasmoneans sometimes tenuous (and their influence is very great).

During the Maccabean revolt, there is considerable persecution of Jews in Galilee. About 160 BCE Simon Maccabeus advances into Galilee, engages the pagans in several battles and drives them off in disorder; he pursues them to the gate of Ptolemais where they lose about three thousand men whose spoils he collects. He takes away with him the Jews of Galilee and Arbatta, with their wives and children and all their possessions, and brings them into Judea with great rejoicing (I Mc 5:21–23). Although the text from Maccabees is not nuanced, it is unlikely that *all* of the Jews of Galilee are relocated; probably those from the outlying areas on the west (Arbatta was a coastal area south of Ptolemais) are taken south for safety. Yet, cut off as it is geographically from the south, Galilee must have remained nervous about its safety. It is not until the end of the second century BCE that Galilee is annexed to the Hasmonean Kingdom; and only then do the Jews who were moved to the south return. Galilee's nervousness is reflected in the decision of Aristobulus, recorded by Josephus, to require that non-Jews who remain in the area must be circumcised and live in keeping with Jewish law (Ant 13:318).

The independence of the Jewish nation ends when the Roman General Pompey is victorious over the King of Pontus in 65 BCE. All of Asia Minor falls under Roman control. Herod is eventually named King by the Romans. When he returns from Rome in 39 BCE he lands at Ptolemais, collects an army, and marches through Galilee with little resistance. Josephus observes that "all Galilee, except a few of its inhabitants, came over to his side" (Ant 14:395; Wars 1:291). After the death of Herod, his son Antipas rules Galilee from 4 BCE to 39 BCE (virtually during the entire life span of Jesus). Judea, however, is placed under the direct control of a Roman procurator, making the political situation of Judea tighter under Roman rule. Let us look at Galilee, before and after the Roman conquest, from the perspective of acculturation to Greek ways.

Hellenization and Galilee

During the period before the Roman occupation, how much is Jewish life in Galilee Hellenized, in what ways, and at what depths? There are important Greek centers all around the perimeter of Galilee, but there is no such settlement within the heart of rural Galilee (Sepphoris is the closest candidate, but it is not a Greek *polis*). Ptolemais is on the coast northwest of Lower Galilee. It is an important commercial port that handles produce from Galilee. But in Freyne's judgment, Ptolemais does not have any significant cultural influence upon Galilee.[11] Scythopolis, the south-southeast of lower Galilee, is a Greek settlement that co-exists easily with Galilee. There were contacts with Galilee, but again, this town did not Hellenize its neighbors.[12] Similar judgments hold for the Greek towns to the west, beyond the Jordan.

Given its power and importance, Tyre (further north on the coast) is the best candidate for a Hellenizing influence, though that does not seem to have been the case either. Tyre was Greek enough to have been host to the Olympic games in 172 BCE. Its citizens had participated in the games in Delos a century before. Ezekiel notes Tyre's commercial ties with Israel and Judah for wax, honey, tallow and balm (Ezk 27:17). It is Freyne's judgment that during the period in question, evidence does not suggest that Tyre causes any large scale cultural change in Galilee.[13]

The question is not whether there was a Greek influence upon Galilean Judaism, but how extensive and what kind it was. After examining one by one the Greek cities around the edges of Galilee, Freyne concludes that "on the whole evidence weighs against those who see the cities as the agents for large-scale cultural change in Galilee" in the pre-Roman period.[14] We must turn attention now to the Roman period.

During the Roman period, some limited urbanization reaches into the center of Galilee in the cities of Sepphoris and Tiberias (the latter founded only in 13 CE). Sepphoris, only a few miles from Nazareth, is ideally situated in a mountainous area to become a fortress. In 57 BCE the Romans make it the seat of a council for Galilee, and it soon has both a bank and an archive. Though a strong town, Sepphoris does not take a stand against the Romans. Freyne suggests that the inhabitants are not so much pro-Roman, but have developed a pacifism.[15] The town is clearly inhabited by Jews, not by Romans. In fact, Rabbinic sources make clear that Sepphoris is a priestly town. The townspeople, however, resist getting involved in all the turmoil that is developing.[16] For whatever reason it is that Sepphoris is not anti-Roman, the rest of Galilee has a continuing animosity toward Sepphoris. In any case, it is certainly the case that Sepphoris does not inculturate Galilee.

It is during the early life of Jesus that Herod Antipas founds the city of Tiberias on the Sea of Galilee, about five miles south of Capernaum. Though administratively it resembles a Greek *polis,* it is largely a town of Jewish aristocrats with a small Greek minority, and with little appeal to Galilee's peasant farmers and fishers.[17] Josephus documents Galilean hatred of both Sepphoris and Tiberias. Jesus of Sapphias, a revolutionary guerrilla leader, and some Galileans kill the small Greek population and burn Herod's palace there. While Tiberias probably adds to the presence of the Greek language in Galilee, there is not enough interaction between Tiberias and the Galilean peasants to have a significant effect on the ethos of rural Galilee.

Freyne examines the cities of the Decapolis and some other Greco-Roman towns, and concludes about them as well that while they helped make the Greek language become more familiar, they do not seem to have inculturated Galilee significantly into the world-view and ethos of Greek culture.

In the latter part of this chapter, I will take up the significance of the issue of Greek language and culture. But for the moment, some assessment can be made about the presence of Greek in Galilee. Unquestionably the Greek language becomes familiar through commercial contacts in Galilee. Numerous inscriptions found by archaeologists give ample testimony for this. Aramaic, however, remains the daily vernacular language of the area. Meyers and Strange note a consensus that the Hebrew language remains a live option, and knowledge of the ancient tongue is never lost.[18] This is basically Freyne's judgment as well. That some significant knowledge of Hebrew continues is no surprise, since Hebrew is regularly taught to young children in the synagogue schools, and there is every reason to presume that this was the practice in Galilee.

Galileans would have needed "some Greek" for commercial purposes (though this is less the case for rural farmers). Learning some Greek for commercial reasons, however, does not acculturate a person very markedly in the

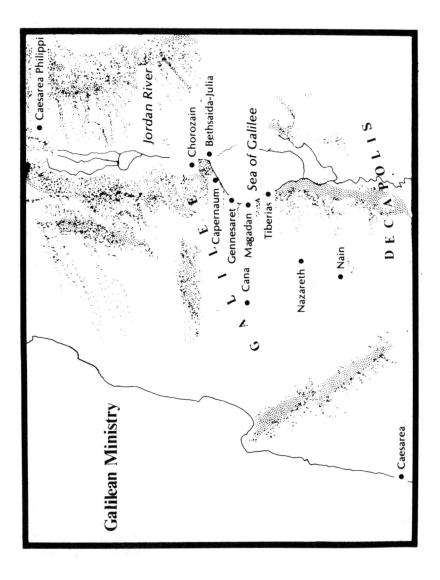

Galilean Ministry

Caesarea Philippi

Jordan River

Chorozain

Bethsaida-Julia

G A L I L E E

Capernaum

Gennesaret

Cana

Magadan

Sea of Galilee

Tiberias

Nazareth

Nain

D E C A P O L I S

Caesarea

world view of a culture. For example, the Mexicans in towns that border the United States often learn enough English to conduct trade, but that commercial use of English does not significantly Americanize their life style, or how their hearts and minds understand the world. That is not the same as studying English, using it in daily ways, learning its literature, its philosophy, etc. That kind of exposure and transformation occurred for Jews who lived in the diaspora in Greek cities, but not in Galilee. Given the cultural ties of Jerusalem to diaspora Judaism, as well as some commercial intercourse, knowledge of Greek was bound to have had a larger influence in the Judaism of southern Palestine than in Galilee. Even so, Jerusalem is no Alexandria.

Jesus' Villages

We have glanced at the more Hellenized cities around the perimeter of Lower Galilee. Now we will take a closer look at the cities of particular interest because we know from the Later Scriptures that they were significant in the life of Jesus: Nazareth, Capernaum, Chorozain, Bethsaida, and some of the regions Jesus visited. These areas are the most immediate context for Jesus' life and work. They provide essential context for the interpretation of this extraordinary life.

Nazareth, Jesus' home, is a small agricultural village in the very heart of rural Galilee. It appears from archeology to have been an ancient settlement which is refounded in the second century BCE.[19] The excavations turn up no evidence of wealth. The size of the settlement suggests a population of between 1,600 and 2,000. There is no mention of Nazareth in any ancient Jewish sources earlier than the third century CE, surely an index of its lack of prominence, and reason, perhaps, for Nathaniel to question whether anything important could come out of Nazareth (Jn 1:46). Meyers and Strange feel it is "clear from circumstantial evidence that Nazareth was a thoroughly Jewish settlement; it was in fact one of the areas where priests resettled after the disaster of 70 CE."[20]

Matthew's Gospel places Jesus, at the beginning of his public life, in Judea with John the Baptist. After the arrest of John the Baptist Jesus leaves Galilee, returns north, and moves from Nazareth to Capernaum (Mt 4:12–13). Capernaum appears to be the center of Jesus' activity during most of his public life, although he does return to Nazareth where he is known as "a hometown boy" (Mt 13:53–58). Vermes judges that Capernaum is not of much importance in Galilee since it is mentioned only once in all of the writings of Josephus, who is deeply interested in Galilee which he knows first-hand.[21] Estimates of the size of Capernaum range from 100,000 square meters (population of 4,000–5,000) to about 325,000 square meters (population of 12,000–15,000). Meyers and Strange tend toward the latter estimate, since it was the seat of a customs house, and seem to make more of Capernaum than Vermes, calling it a "teeming Jewish commercial and agricultural center [and thus perhaps] a natural selection for Jesus' headquarters."[22] I gather, however, that the customs house may only indicate that Capernaum is the first town within the jurisdiction of Antipas coming from the north. Meyers and Strange indicate that so far in the excavations no public buildings have been found, and that would suggest to me something less than a teeming center. Of course further excavations may alter that judgment. On the basis of either estimate about size and relative importance, Capernaum was not a major center by any stretch of the imagination. It was a prosperous fishing town and undoubtedly had some agriculture. If Jesus had been looking for a teeming center, or as close as you can get to that in rural Galilee, Sepphoris would have been the logical choice, or perhaps Tiberias further south.

Similar judgments are to be made about Bethsaida and Chorozain. They are smaller villages for whom fishing and some agriculture are the basis of livelihood. The three towns where much of Jesus' public life is spent would seem to be relatively untouched by any deep cultural syncretism with Greek culture. They are not centers of any kind, like Sepphoris or Tiberias. They are very rural in character. Vermes is inclined to speak of the "overwhelming Jewishness" of these areas in the time of Jesus.[23] He even suggests a sort of Galilean chauvinism that may be responsible for what seems to be Jesus' antipathy toward the Gentiles, and feels about Jesus that "at heart, he was a real campagnard . . . at home among the simple people of rural Galilee."[24]

The mystery, if there is one, is why Sepphoris is not a recipient of the teaching and preaching of Jesus. One can only guess. It is surely curious that this important city, just a few miles from Nazareth, does not make an appearance in the Gospels. It does not seem unreasonable that Jesus' reasons for avoiding Sepphoris would have been inherited from his own rural culture in Nazareth, for reasons given above. Recall also the antipathy toward Sepphoris that expresses itself at Herod's death in 4 BCE. Judas, the son of Hezikiah, gathers a group substantial enough to attack the city and raid the royal arsenal. For this rebellious act, the Roman Varus destroys the city. Herod Antipas not only rebuilds it but does so with such finesse that Josephus calls it "the ornament of all Galilee" (Ant 18:27).

Jesus and the House of Israel, and Religious Particularism

What I think becomes clear in this picture of Galilee is, as Vermes indicates, its overwhelming Jewishness. One of the remarkable and clear pieces of evidence from the Gospels about the behavior of Jesus is that he systematically avoids the Greek cities. When he goes to Nazareth, Capernaum, Bethsaida, Chorozain, and Jerusalem there is no question that he goes *into* those cities and towns. The careful wording of Gospel passages makes the point clear that he did not go into the town of Gedara, only the *countryside* (*eis ten choran*). The people there are frightened by Jesus' presence and ask him to leave their *neighborhood* (*apo ton horion auton*) (Mk 5:1–18). Jesus sets out for *the regions* of Tyre and then returns from *those regions* via the *region* of the Decapolis (Mk 7:24–31). Jesus and the disciples leave for "the villages *around* Caesarea Philippi" (Mk 8:27). Jesus encounters the Syro-Phoenician woman when he withdraws to the *region* of Tyre and Sidon. To be sure, there is no literal report from Jesus about the "why" of these behaviors. But it is a reasonable supposition that his own sense of living and teaching as a Jew among and for Jews is a likely reason for Jesus' avoidance of less provincially Jewish places.

There is no evidence in the synoptics that Jesus has a sense of mission to the Gentiles. The mandate to go to all the nations, at the end of Matthew's Gospel, is generally accepted as a development in the church's sense of mission and is not an original saying of Jesus. [Even the reference to the Samaritan woman in John's Gospel probably reflects the mission expansion of the early church rather than a biographical event.[25]] Jesus instructs the Twelve: "Do not make your way to Gentile territory, and do not enter any Samaritan town; go instead to the lost sheep of the House of Israel" (Mt 10:5). These words represent Jesus' directives to his followers.

Jesus' own sense of his personal mission appears to be similar. When he is in the region of Tyre and Sidon, a woman from that area begins shouting to him for her daughter's cure. Jesus ignores her. The disciples plead with Jesus to pay attention to her so she will leave them alone. Jesus replies: "I was sent only to the lost sheep of the House of Israel. . . . It is not fair to take the children's food and throw it to little dogs." But she persists, and Jesus grants her request: "Woman, you have great faith. Let your desire be granted" (Mt 15:21:28). John Meier suggests that the handling of this passage "reflects a complicated historical process whereby a stringently Jewish-Christian community opened itself up to a gentile mission."[26] Geza Vermès, however, feels that "the authenticity of these sayings must be well nigh impregnable, taking into account their shocking inappropriateness in an internationally open

Church."[27] Both observations make a valid point. Once Christians understand themselves in terms of a universal mission, a struggle unresolved in Matthew, these "only to the House of Israel" texts would probably be an embarrassment. I do not think that "only to the House of Israel" is a deliberate theological composition by a church with a sense of universal mission. I take these words to be historical reminiscences, even as the "handling" of them, as Meier suggests, reflects a development in the Christian community's sense of itself.

Another incident has similar overtones. Jesus goes into the countryside of Gadara, a Hellenized city on the other side of the Sea of Galilee, and cures a possessed man there. When the cured man asks to remain with Jesus, Jesus does not accept him into his following. He sends him back: "Go home to your people and tell them all that the Lord in his mercy has done for you" (Mk 5:17,29). Jesus never turned down any Jew who wanted to be a follower.

Almost as a footnote to this section, I want to speak to the larger issue of religious particularism (only to the House of Israel) and universalism (baptize all nations). Christians have sometimes asserted the claim that Christianity differentiates itself from Judaism as a universalism over and against a particularism, i.e., that in Christian universalism, Jewish particularism is transcended. The great religious traditions of the world all show marked tensions between particularism and universalism. That was true of the ancient Jewish tradition. It was true of Judaism in the time of Jesus. It is true of Judaism today. It was true for Christians in the earliest communities. It is true for Christian churches today.

In the courtroom of history, no one of the major religious traditions of the world has simultaneously been able to surrender all vestiges of religious imperialism and yet retain an effective, compelling and generous summons to total commitment within its tradition. Traditions make ideological claims about their universalism, but in concrete history no religious tradition has yet functioned that way. I agree strongly with John Cobb that while we may yet, in ecumenical dialogue, have to name our differences honestly and clearly, a major task is to move "beyond dialogue" about conflicting claims to finality.[28] The "beyond" is simply an open relationship. When any two people listen intently to each other's experience, not for the sake of argument or dialogue, but solely for the sake of understanding one another more fully, both parties are inevitably changed by having received the experience of an "other." Transformation by the experience of another does not necessarily mean agreement. But it does mean enlargement of the spirit through having had to stretch to take in otherness.

The particularism/universalism struggle is endemic to monotheistic faith.

If there is but one Ultimate Reality, it must be everyone's Ultimate Reality. Everyone's Creator. Everyone's Father/Mother. Every Atman's access to Brahman. Every disciple's way to Enlightenment/Buddha. Every person's path to Allah. Everyone's Yahweh. Every encounter with Ultimacy is thoroughly conditioned and even mediated through the particularities of our histories, our cultures, our individual personalities. Every encounter with Ultimacy, therefore, has on it the *trademark* of a particular tradition—there is no meta-cultural, "generic," *un-trademarked* experience of Deity. The danger is always that the *trademark* assumes ideological finality—a claim more fruitfully left to the adjudication of history.

I do not question the claim of faith that a particular Way offers the *possibility* of calling us to become a single human family (which could never mean the suppression of cultural differentiation), and that such a Way is a response to God's initiative. In fact, I want to make this *possibility* be part of the Christian claim. But the possible must not be confused with the concretely actual. In this regard, the tensed way of living between religious particularism and religious universalism, between claim and fact, continues to mark both Jewish and Christian experience.

Jesus Beyond the House of Israel, and Hints at Religious Universalism

Although I do not see evidence that Jesus understood himself to have stepped outside of his own Jewish faith, I do believe there is evidence of tension between particularism and universalism in Jesus' experience. Therefore, I want to continue briefly this exploration of the Jewish particularism out of which and thanks to which Christian particularisms emerge. For Christian particularism shares with Jewish particularism an inner urge toward the de-tribalization of deity. The issue about Jesus' Jewishness may seem to Jews too obvious to belabor. But to Christians who have tenacious traditions of piety and doctrine which insist that Jesus consciously intended to found a church that superseded Judaism, it is worth sitting with evidence, not just positing a claim.

Jesus observes the religious customs of the Jews, from going to the synagogue on the sabbath (often teaching there—Mk 1:21) to traveling to the Temple in Jerusalem for Passover. Jesus pays the half shekel tax that is levied on each Jew for the upkeep of the Temple (Mt 17:24–27). After curing a leper, Jesus sends him to the priest to make the healing offering prescribed by Moses (Mk 1:44). And even the fierce polemics with the Pharisees in Matthew (Mt 23) begin with Jesus' affirmation that the Pharisees do indeed sit in the chair of Moses, and should be heard and obeyed even if their example is not always to be followed (Mt 23:1–3). We surely encounter in Matthew 23 the conflicts of the early community after the destruction of the Temple, yet the affirmation of the legitimacy of the Oral Tradition seems likely to reflect the bearing of Jesus.

Notwithstanding all I have said about the Jewishness of Jesus and the particularism of its Galilean configuration, we do indeed see issues surface in Jesus' life about the universality of God and its effects upon the universe of humankind. Faith is a category that names one as an "insider," as it were, to a redeeming relationship with God. In both Earlier and Later Scriptures, faith is above all an issue of the heart which is the fundamental locus of the work of God's Spirit. Jesus would, of course, expect to find faith in Nazareth, a thoroughly Jewish town. But Matthew says that Jesus did not work many miracles in Nazareth because of their lack of faith (Mt 13:38). Matthew has softened the account which he took over from Mark's Gospel. Mark says more strongly that Jesus was unable to work miracles there (except for a few cures), and he was amazed at their lack of faith (Mk 6:5–6). Jesus does work many miracles among his people, so it is certainly true that sometimes he finds faith and sometimes he doesn't; he is painfully surprised when he doesn't, however. He tells the Jewish woman with the hemorrhage that he cures her precisely because she does have faith.

In the very incident in which Jesus tells the Canaanite woman that he has come only for the Jews, she continues to plead and argue with him for the cure of her daughter until it becomes clear to Jesus that he has found a woman with strong faith outside of Israel. " 'Woman, you have great faith. Let your desire be granted.' And from that moment her daughter was well again" (Mt 15:28). Jesus finds genuine faith outside of Israel.

Similarly, and strikingly, Jesus encounters a Roman centurion asking for the cure of his servant. He tells Jesus that there is no need for Jesus to come to his house, but " 'just give the word and my servant will be cured.' . . . When Jesus heard this he was astonished [at faith in a pagan] and said to those following him, 'In truth I tell you, in no one in Israel have I found faith as great as this. And I tell you that many will come from east and west and sit down with Abraham and Isaac and Jacob at the feast in the kingdom of Heaven; but the children of the kingdom will be thrown out into the darkness outside, where there will be weeping and grinding of teeth.' And to the centurion Jesus said, 'Go back, then; let this be done for you, as your faith demands.' And the servant was cured at that moment" (Mt 8:5–13).

The very same verb is used in this passage from Matthew to express amazement at finding faith outside of Israel that is used in Mark to express Jesus' surprise at the lack of faith within Israel. Now there is surely in this passage an overlay of the struggle of the early communities to deal with followers of Jesus who are not Jewish. But the major point is the astonished discovery of Jesus that faith transcends the particularism where it was first experienced and where one naturally, therefore, most expects to find it. God's saving presence cannot be fenced in by any particularism, Jewish, Christian, or any other kind. For Jesus and for Christians, the Fatherhood [the universal parenthood] of God becomes a key metaphor for understanding how faith can be universal. The Fatherhood of God is not absent in the faith of the Earlier Scriptures; God is directly named as Father about a dozen times (though implied much more often). In the Earlier Scriptures, however, the role of God as Creator is the most detribalized way of naming deity. In the Christian faith, the universal parenthood of God is not just another motif, but the leit-motif for faith's full orchestration.

The early polemics between Christians and Jews are more complex than arguments about particularism and universalism, but those arguments are one layer of contention. Sometimes the contentiousness between Jews and Christians has the kind of fierceness that can only be observed in conflict between siblings. Jesus was and is and ever shall be fully Jewish, a fact (in my judgment) that must be honored in every version of Christian faith. Such honoring is an act of fidelity to the Fourth Commandment, for we Christians are Jewish children. We may not be only that, but we are never less than that or other than that. This conviction does not, finally, jeopardize what emerges as a distinctive structure of Christian life. But it does jeopardize many of the ways we have interpreted our distinctiveness. We are richest when we are truest to every part of ourselves. Our systematic distancing of ourselves from our Jewishness over the centuries has not only worked shameful havoc upon our Jewish brothers and sisters, it has deprived us of some of the world's most moving resources for our faith.

Galilee and the Revolutionaries

As we continue to converse with the Jesus-event, and seek to hear Jesus speak out of a thick history, there is yet another matter of towering concern. It is a deeply disturbing issue. While still a relatively young man, Jesus was arrested, tried, convicted, sentenced and executed. Why? The Gospel accounts all indicate collusion between Jewish religious leaders and Roman authorities. Now I have been stressing the genetic connections between Jesus and his Jewish faith. If there were deep differences between Jesus and religious leadership, what were the issues? It is generally acknowledged today that much of the polemic between Jesus and the Pharisees is the argument of the early church read back into Jesus' life. Whatever historical differences there were between Jesus and the Pharisees, they cannot be a sufficient explanation for Jewish collusion with the Romans in the death of a Jew. That then heightens our concern for the political mood at the time, and especially for an assessment of what some call the ''revolutionary ethos'' of Galilee. How much ''revolution'' is in the air in the time of Jesus?

The situation that unfolds under Roman control is crucial. Resistance to the Romans is a quite different experience than resistance to the Seleucids. The Hasmoneans fought the Seleucids in the waning years of their power. But in the first centuries BCE and CE Roman power is at its zenith, and the Jews do not really have a chance at all at successful revolt. It is a painful time, and the pain is usually seething below the surface since so little can actually be effected in power realignment.

Recall the Maccabean foray into Galilee to rescue its citizens. They are taken south, and return only toward the end of the second century BCE. For obvious reasons the Galilean repatriates are fiercely protective of their Jewishness. It is barely forty years later when Rome becomes the powerful new overlord. At the time when Pompey conquers Syria from King Pontus, and then turns to the Jews, a Hasmonean conflict is going on among the Jews themselves, between Aristobulus II and Hyrcanus II (Salome's sons). That provides just the excuse for Pompey to intervene. In 63 BCE Pompey makes Hyrcanus II the High Priest, and Aristobulus flees to Rome with his family, including his son Antigonus. Pompey gives administrative direction of the Jews to an Idumenean convert, Antipater. When Antipater is poisoned in 43 BCE, his sons, Herod and Phasael are left in charge of Judea. Aristobulus' son Antigonus returns from Roman exile to try to re-establish Hasmonean hegemony. For a short time he is able to take control of the country.

Herod in the meantime goes to Rome, has himself proclaimed King, returns, gathers an army in the north, easily marches through Galilee, reconquers Judea, and after a five month campaign manages to retake and pillage (except for the Temple) Jerusalem. To try to gain Jewish credibility, Herod marries Mariamne, the granddaughter of Hyrcanus II whom he had appointed high priest—but in his paranoia over palace intrigue, he has her and her two sons killed. The magnificent construction he added to the Temple in Jerusalem is still another attempt to make some Roman peace with the Jews. (It is also a further expression of his legendary megalomania demonstrated in the huge scale of his building projects in Hebron, at Masada, and his Herodian palace/fortress in the Judean desert.)

At Herod's death in 4 BCE, control passes to his three sons, two in the north and Archeleus in Judea. In 6 CE Augustus removes Archeleus and places the south directly under Roman control. The Galilee of Jesus escapes direct Roman control, and remains under Herod Antipas, the son of Herod the Great. This all too brief historical summary brings us up to the time of Jesus, and helps elicit a concrete sense of the world in which he lived. Unquestionably during the lifetime of Jesus, there is general and sometimes vicious discontent with Roman rule in Palestine. Is Galilee a hotbed of revolutionary passion? Vermes makes a rather strong case for this, suggesting that "the struggle against the empire was nevertheless not just a family business, but a full-scale Galilean activity in the first century."[29] Freyne feels that the revolutionary fever is far more moderate in Galilee. He sees Judea as the locale for the stronger political animus and judges that "very little of this intense feeling comes to the fore in Galilee, with the exception of the destitute classes of Tiberias in 66 CE."[30] The question cannot be settled unambiguously, but we will look at some of the clues. I do not intend to treat the question of whether or not Jesus himself was a political revolutionary, or whether he belonged to the rather violent Zealot party. I think the answer is clearly no, and that this issue has been fairly treated.[31] Whether Jesus might have been perceived by Roman authority as a political threat is still another question, one that must be addressed.

How revolutionary? Let us consider both of the assessments cited above. What favors the likelihood of a rather vigorous revolutionary ethos in Galilee? Consider what almost seems like a Galilean "dynasty" of violent resistance.

Herod is only fifteen when his father Antipater leaves Galilee to his rule. Josephus writes that "his youth in no way hindered him. . . . For on learning that Hezekias, a bandit leader, was overwhelming the borders of Syria with a large troop, he caught and killed him, and many of the bandits with him" (Ant 14:158–159). When Herod dies, Hezekias' son Judas takes revenge by attacking Sepphoris with a considerable band of followers, plundering the royal arsenals and treasury (War 2:56). This may well be the same Judas as the one known as Judas the Galilean and Judas of Gamala, who leads Jews in the south to rebel when Quirinus orders an assessment of Jewish property for tax purposes. Judas, together with a Pharisee named Sadok, founds a new party, the Zealots, which Josephus, in Greek categories, calls a "fourth philosophy" (along with Pharisees, Sadducees and Essenes). Josephus characterizes the Zealots as follows:

> As for the fourth of the philosophies, Judas the Galilean set himself up as leader of it. This school agrees in all other respects with the opinions of the Pharisees, except that they have a passion for liberty that is almost unconquerable, since they are convinced that God alone is their leader and master.

They think little of submitting to death in unusual forms and permitting vengeance to fall on kinsmen and friends if only they may avoid calling any
man master. In as much as most people have seen the steadfastness of their
resolution amid such circumstances, I may forgo any further account. For I
have no fear that anything reported of them will be considered incredible.
The danger is, rather, that report may minimize the indifference with which
they accept the grinding misery of pain (Ant 18:23–24).

Josephus probably exaggerates the fierceness of the Zealots for his own ag-
grandizement, since he once had a leadership role in Galilee and had to deal
with them. Yet, as Marcel Simon observes in his study of Jewish sects, ''it is
difficult to believe that he has completely distorted them. The wretchedness in
which they lived probably had something to do with their agitation, which
would thus be the expression, in certain aspects, of the reaction of what could
be called a proletariat, mainly rural. . . . Whatever their obviously complex
motives, the Zealots were terrorists.''[32]

Josephus further records that the two sons of Judas, Jacob and Simon, are
later crucified for rebellious activity (Ant 20:102). Still a third son, Menahem,
''took intimate friends off with him to Masada, where he broke into King Herod's armoury and provided arms for his fellow-townsmen and for other brig-
ands; then, with these men for his bodyguard, he returned like a veritable king
to Jerusalem, became the leader of the revolution, and directed the siege of the
palace'' (War 2:434). Menahem is found in his place of hiding, ''caught,
dragged into the open, and after being subjected to all kinds of torture, put to
death'' (War 2:448). However, one of Menahem's relatives, Eleazar, escapes
to Masada and there, in the fortress built on a mountain top beside the Dead
Sea, becomes the legendary leader of the Zealots who finally elected mass su-
icide rather than capitulate to the Romans. Even if many of the events named
did not occur on Galilean territory, it would have been natural to recognize the
Galilean origin of the Zealots and the Galilean roots of revolutionary leaders
and terrorists.

On the other hand, Freyne feels that the religious activity in Galilee is not
seriously threatened, and that resistance there would not be at white heat. The
Zealots are but one of several groups, and not a very large one.[33] The kind of
eschatological fervor that would fuel violence and terrorism, Freyne feels, is
more a characteristic of Judea in the south, and that such intense feeling does
not characterize the more peasant ethos of Galilee. He agrees with Simon that
Josephus surely exaggerated the power of the Zealots for his own purposes.

Clearly, we cannot assess with certainty what the revolutionary temper of
Galilee was like in Jesus' time. But I am inclined to believe that it was sig-

nificant. When the Sanhedrin is deliberating what to do with the post-Easter followers of Jesus, Gamaliel draws a comparison between Jesus and Judas the Galilean, saying that time and history will decide whether Jesus is from God (Acts 5:34–39). The memory of revolution is there in Gamaliel. During the active life of Jesus in Galilee, some people arrive, apparently concerned for Jesus' safety, and report that Pilate had some Galilean Jews killed in Jerusalem, and mingled their blood with the blood of their sacrifices (Lk 13:1). Perhaps even more telling is Josephus' account of the death of John the Baptist, different in detail from the Gospel account:

> [John the Baptist] was a good man who exhorted the Jews to lead righteous lives, to practice justice toward their fellows and piety toward God. . . . When others too joined the crowds about him, because they were aroused to the highest degree by his sermons, Herod became alarmed. Eloquence that had so great an effect on mankind *might lead to some form of sedition,* for it looked as if they would be guided by John in everything they did. Herod decided that it would be much better to strike first and be rid of him before his work led to an uprising, than to wait for an upheaval, get involved in a difficult situation and see his mistake. (Ant 18:117–118, emphasis added)

Even though John's message was clearly religious, Herod had him killed because *he might have been* a rallying point for violent crowds. Mark records that when Herod heard about Jesus, he opined that John the Baptist had come back to life (Mk 6:14–16). We are probably, of course, not catching the live words of Herod; but I think we are catching a mood and an association. It is impossible to miss the similarity between Jesus and everything Josephus said about John the Baptist, and to recognize the possibility that the same thing that got John in trouble was a major factor in the death of Jesus. Although it is not a topic that I shall address, I want to indicate my general agreement with Ellis Rivkin's recent study of the crucifixion of Jesus, that the felt threat of Jesus was political, and that responsibility for the arrest and execution of Jesus belongs primarily with the Romans. The high priest is appointed by the Romans, not selected by the Jews. Retention of the high priesthood depends upon the high priest's cooperation with the Romans.[34]

If Jesus' activity resembled John's in a clearly volatile moment of history, his preoccupation with the Kingdom of God would also be easily misread by the Romans. For Jesus, Kingdom and Kingship are central symbols of God's promise. "King," therefore, is a very nervous word in the mouth of any Jewish public figure, and "Kingdom of God" is a recurring theme in the teaching of Jesus. "The possibility must have been very real," Freyne says, "that Jesus' audience would have understood his message and the symbols he used to express it in political terms.''[35] While there is no evidence in the Gospels that Jesus ever spoke in a political way about the Kingdom, there is evidence that he was understood that way, both by the crowds that wanted to make him king and even by his more intimate following.

It may not be clear how to measure the revolutionary ethos on a scale of one to ten; but it is clear that these are edgy times indeed, and that an image fundamental to Jesus' teaching—that of Kingdom—is politically loaded. The Kingdom of God is a familiar theme in the Judaism of Jesus. And when such a theme is center stage in the teachings of a charismatic figure, the body politic is bound to have a nervous stomach. Rivkin's words are quite to the point:

> In such a world, where violence stalked the countryside, death frequented the streets of Jerusalem, and riots disturbed the precincts of the Temple; where every flutter of dissidence sent chills of fear up the spines of puppet kings, governors, procurators, and procurator appointed high priests—even the most nonpolitical of charismatics took his life in his own hands when he preached the good news of God's coming Kingdom. And if his call to repentance were so eloquent that crowds gathered round to hear and to hope, would not the power of his word invite the kiss of death?[36]

In such an atmosphere as we find in Palestinian Judaism at this time, it is my guess that Jesus must have felt the power of the symbol of Kingdom, within himself and for his hearers. It would be risky to capitalize on such a volatile symbol. Yet if the political passion that clothes it can be transferred to religious expectation, a response worthy of Ultimacy is in the making.

Greek and Hebrew: Cultural Contrasts About Ultimate Reality

The theologian Bernard Loomer frequently told a ''bottom elephant'' story to his students. A disciple approaches his guru to ask what for him is a pressing question, ''The world is so very large; what holds it up?'' The guru asks for a little time for meditation first, and then tells his disciple, ''It rests upon the back of a large elephant.'' The disciple is satisfied for a while, but returns to ask, ''What do the feet of the large elephant rest upon?'' After a longer meditation this time, the guru says, ''Its feet are upon an even larger world than the world on its back.'' The disciple accepts that, but soon returns, and then returns again, and then again, to find each time a larger elephant upon a larger world, upon a far larger elephant, upon a far larger world, etc. When the guru is on his death bed, the disciple asks, ''Please, tell me what the bottom elephant stands on?'' Drawing his final breath, the guru says, ''If I knew that, I would know everything!'' Loomer's point is that every system of thought rests upon presuppositions, which in turn rest upon nothing else: they are bottom elephants.

I share Paul Ricoeur's conviction that bottom elephants are symbols and not propositional statements, and that our knowing arises from a metaphorical grasp of the world around us.[37] Bottom elephant metaphors are root metaphors, that is, they are the starting point for a whole narrative structure, a whole way of putting life's story together. Major cultural differences are at base a contrast in bottom elephant metaphors. Because there are such fundamental contrasts between the Hebrew and the Greek story, I have been at pains to suggest that even though there is clearly a notable impact of Greek ways upon Hebrew ways in Palestine in the time of Jesus, the impact does not get down to the level of bottom elephant metaphors. Jesus may well have known some Greek, but when he says ''God,'' ''Word,'' ''Spirit,'' ''world,'' ''truth,'' etc., we must have recourse to a Hebrew world view to interpret their meaning and their consequences in his experience and in ours if we are to hear Jesus on his own ground.

I shall indicate in volume two that in the Wisdom tradition, there is some ''rub off'' from Greek thought on the very foundations of Jewish thought. And this is even truer of the *logos* tradition of John's Gospel, and still earlier in Philo. When Philo said ''God,'' Stoic and Platonic bottom elephants supported its meaning world. In his classical study of *Judaism,* George Foot Moore says that Philo's theology really exerted ''no discoverable influence in the main current of Jewish thought.''[38] That is particularly so of Galilean Jewish thought in Jesus' time. Authentic conversation with the Jesus-event requires that we work our tedious way through layers and layers of interpretation to understand his bottom elephants, as best we can.

Jewish Root Metaphors in Hellenized Palestine

I have indicated already many of the historical and geographical reasons why I believe that Hellenism does not invade Palestinian Judaism at the level of foundational metaphors, especially in Galilee, but largely so in Judea as well. The Hasmonean revolt is against the attempted enforcement of Hellenism by Antiochus Epiphanes (who has the help of sympathetic Jewish Hellenizers). The Pharisaic movement allows the Jews to reinterpret their covenantal commitments so as to come to terms with the political realities of Greek and Roman power. The Pharisees themselves are a sort of academy of scholars. But the ''logic'' of the pharisaic ''academy'' has little in common with the rational tradition of the Greek academy. After the terrible destruction of the temple in 70 CE, the leading Pharisees leave Jerusalem and settle in Yavneh, near the Mediterranean almost due west of Jerusalem. Here, as Robert Selzer observes, "a rabbinic blueprint for Jewish survival was articulated."[39] This gathering is the new Sanhedrin for the Jews in Palestine. Here the oral tradition starts to be gathered and written down, the canon of the scriptures is determined, prayers are given a more definite form. The daily language is Aramaic, and the texts that are undergoing formulation are in Hebrew. It is worth noting that the book of the Wisdom of Solomon, composed in Greek in Alexandria about 50 BCE, is not included in the Jewish canon. (The Christian tradition includes it, and uses its materials to help interpret the christological meaning of Jesus.)

Like the Hasmonean "No" to Hellenization in 164 BCE, two centuries later the Bar Kokhba War in 132 CE is a revolt against Emperor Hadrian's championing of Hellenism. The Roman response is devastating. Hadrian forbids the practice of Judaism. This prohibition is revoked in 138 CE by his successor, Emperor Antoninus Pius. After the revolt, the Sanhedrin regathers in Galilee, in the town of Usha (near the present site of Haifa). It is here that Judaism's important religious classic, the Mishnah, is composed. It is written in fluent Hebrew. Moore finds the Mishnah and the two Talmuds which continue the interpretive tasks of the Mishnah to be virtually without any traces of Greek thought.[40]

I am suggesting that the rabbinic decision to go down a fully Hebraic road is consonant with and disclosive of the deeper impulses that characterized Palestinian Judaism throughout most of its contact with Hellenism. I read this rabbinic choice backward in support of my contention that Palestinian Judaism was not very permeable to Greek influence at the level of bottom elephants. That the rabbinic choice was not the Greek road is clear. In his remarkable work on rabbinic teaching, Ephraim Urbach notes that "the Sages [the rabbinic successors of the Pharisees] were not acquainted with Greek philosophy, and not one of its great representatives is mentioned anywhere in Rabbinic literature except Epicurus in Sanhedrin X,1. . . . "[41] And even here, Epicurus is mentioned as someone who has no share in the world to come. Not incidentally, indeed, it is basically during this very same period, the second century CE, that Christian communities start their journey up a Greek road paved with Stoic, Platonic and Aristotelian worlds of meaning.

In the great formative periods of both Christianity and modern Judaism, different choices were made about different roads to take. The road with the most Jewish traffic became for Christians the less travelled road, or for all practical purposes the abandoned road. The rabbinic materials provide important information about Jesus' time because they do sometimes accurately reflect history. However, they are helpful for another reason as well when we try to hear the voice of Jesus on its own ground. Mishnah, Midrash and Talmud are natural unfoldings of a Jewish trajectory that began at least with the Hasmoneans and the Pharisees, but perhaps as far back as Ezra proclaiming the Torah after the Exile. It is a tenacious Jewish choice, from Ezra right down through the formation of the Mishnah and the Palestinian Talmud. There is some integrity to the road that got travelled, and Jesus was on it in his own time—not a solitary Jewish figure at all, but "one of his own kind," as it were. We must explore the symbolic structures of those contrasting ways or roads.

Jew and Greek: Contrasting Root Metaphors

A metaphoric grasp of reality precedes reflection and rational speculation. When thought arises, it illuminates but never exhausts symbol and metaphor. Once a fable's moral has been understood, the fable's communicative task is over. But a "symbol does not conceal any hidden teaching that only needs to be unmasked for the images in which it is clothed to become useless."[42] Foundational symbols and root metaphors are inexhaustible mines.

At the conclusion of his comparative study of Greek and Hebrew thought, Thorlief Boman offers the following observation:

> The matter is outlined in bold relief by two characteristic figures; the thinking Socrates and the praying Orthodox Jew. When Socrates was seized by a problem, he remained immobile for an interminable period of time in deep thought; when Holy Scripture is read aloud in the synagogue, the Orthodox Jew moves his whole body ceaselessly in deep devotion and adoration. The Greek most acutely experiences the world and existence while he stands and reflects, but the Israelite reaches his zenith in ceaseless movement. Rest, harmony, composure, and self-control—this is the Greek way; movement, life, deep emotion, and power—this is the Hebrew way.[43]

I indicated in the first chapter that interpretation is not only how we grasp a past event, but in the very grasping our interpretation makes possible worlds stand up out in front of us. Put more crassly (and somewhat inadequately), interpretation generates possible behaviors. The Greek in pursuit of contact with Ultimacy is still, because what is Ultimate is motionless and timeless. Augustine, writing in the Greek mode, says in the *Confessions* that time is the measure of motion. If God is immutable, then God is motionless, and therefore radically non-temporal. God is of a different metaphysical order than finite, created beings, as is reflected in the language of "natural" and "supernatural," or "mutable/changeful" and "immutable/changeless." Over the centuries, the Hebrew in pursuit of contact with Ultimacy is in motion: David dancing, and Jews swaying in prayer before the wailing wall in Jerusalem in our own time. For the Jew, God is identified, or defined, if you will, in the language of time: the God of Abraham, Isaac, and Jacob, Yahweh who led us out of Egypt. Admittedly, there are elements of caricature, for we have not described every Greek and every Jew; but these are fundamental contrasts between mainstream Jewish and Greek presuppositions about God.

Here is still another way the contrast has sometimes been described. The Greek understands in a very visual way, the Jew in an aural/oral way.[44] In Greek some of the verb forms that mean "to know" are related to the verb that means "to see." And even the word for "idea" comes from the "see" verb. The Greek wants to see each thing clearly, for exactly what it is. The word for truth, *aletheia,* means unveiling something, taking it out of hiddenness and into the light. Clarity of understanding is achieved by abstraction—the *essential* is abstracted from the *accidentals.*

Greeks show a strong fascination with shape and form, as is clear from their achievement in architecture and sculpture. Greek geometry is equally a fascination with form; and Greek logic itself is a concern for the formal structure of reason apart from any particular content.

In the Hebrew scriptures, there is a near total lack of interest in formal description for its own sake. Hebrew thought is interested in events, not things. Temporality is taken for granted.

In Hellenized Christian theology, the world is a sacrament of God because the created thing resembles the Creator. There is an analogy of being. Sacramentality is not a Hebrew concept. Still, the world does disclose God because it has been *spoken* into reality by God, and God is there in the spoken word. The Hebrew word for "thing" is *dabhar,* and is derived from the verb "to speak." But we must be careful in this case not to think of "thing" in the characteristic English sense of the word. In Hebrew, a "thing" is an event brought into being by speaking—and the speaker is in the event that speaking causes. God *spoke* creation into existence, and still speaks it into existence, so that its being is in the event category and not the thing category. Hebrew shows a deeply historicized preoccupation with events. Further, events are relational. There is no indication of a Hebrew judgment that anything could be real and non-relational at the same time. God, who is most real, is most deeply and truly interactive.

I want to indicate three significant contrasts between the Hebrew and Greek understandings of Ultimate reality. The first has to do with change, the second with the kind of categories that are used to name deity, the third with the issue of ambiguity. I will elaborate the third one a little more fully.

God and Change

First, for a Greek, being that is perfect must be changeless. The logic is simple: to become more tomorrow than I am today means that I am not perfect now. To become less means that my being is degenerable, and that is not perfect. Or simply to be able to become other than I am means that I am not now all that is possible. Perfect being has all that it can have, is all that it can be. It is essentially changeless. It has real effects, but does not receive real effects (those that make a difference in being). Because perfect being has no need, it has no eros. Because it cannot be moved in a way that shapes its concrete reality, there is no real pathos. There is no genuine mutuality between God and the world, because mutuality means interdependence. Perfect being cannot be dependent being—not even interdependent being—because dependence is a limitation. What is Ultimate must stand alone.

The only God with whom Hebrew experience traffics is the God who is with them in history. The marvel and majesty of God are outsized, perhaps: there is no human greatness like God's. But this difference is not metaphysical. The mutuality between God and human history is real. God offers the world a way to tell its story that will redeem it. The story is that of Covenant. But only the *accepted* offer makes redemption be concretely real. We can say No. God can cajole, persuade, and rage, but is finally helpless before the sin of a human "No!" The effective power of God in the world is limited by human freedom. This dependence and sometime helplessness is not an imperfection in Hebrew anthropology, but rather a fullness. Love is vulnerable, and full love is fully vulnerable.

Because God has vested interests in how human history goes, there is satisfaction in God when it goes well for those God loves. There is, then, in God, a kind of eros.[45] Further, God is understood to have feelings about us, and to be moved by those feelings about us. In a word, as Abraham Heschel has written so movingly, the *pathos* of God is real. "Man is rebellious and full of iniquity, and yet so cherished is he that God, the Creator of Heaven and Earth is saddened when forsaken by him."[46] God's happiness is partly dependent upon us, and that is the vulnerability of love's fullness.

Heschel says that the Hebrew prophets know what to say to God's people because they feel the feelings God has for us (a point that will be developed more fully in the next chapter). Only a God who can be moved can have pathos. Heschel observed that "God himself is described as reflecting on the plight of man rather than as contemplating eternal ideas . . . preoccupied . . . with the concrete actualities of history rather than with the timeless issues of thought."[47] There are those, of course, who say that reflections like this are only our faulty anthropomorphisms. I would say rather that pathos is a basic metaphor that mediates and articulates the Hebrew experience of God. "Pathos," of course, is certainly a human word for a human experience, and therefore an anthropomorphism. I agree with Henry Slonimsky's remark in his analysis of Midrash, that "anthropomorphisms [are] devices of the intelligence to say mythologically what we are afraid or unable to say in bald, abstract prose."[48]

Why all this detail? To interpret the meaning of Jesus accurately means hearing him on his own ground. I am suggesting that when he says "God" it is a thoroughly Hebrew meaning that rings in his ears, and that for most of Western theology, when *we* hear Jesus say God, it is a quite Greek meaning that we hear. For a Greek, there is a metaphysical divide between God and human beings that can only be crossed through the contravening invitation of God (to deny that is the Pelagian heresy). For a Jew, God and the world are naturally together and interactive. For the Greek, distancing oneself from all the particularities of history is part of our movement toward God: "Human affairs," said Plato, "are hardly worth considering in earnest, and yet we must be earnest about them: a sad necessity constrains us."[49] The Jew, in one single embrace, can wrap his or her arms around God and human history simultaneously.

The Naming of God

A second point of contrast between Greek and Hebrew is in the naming of Ultimate reality. Again, as Heschel illustrates, the Greek mind asks "What is God?" and responds with *formal* answers that are familiar to classical Christian theism. Formal answers are abstract characteristics of God's essence: God is immutable—cannot change. God is omnipotent—there is nothing (except logical contradiction) that God cannot do. God is omniscient—never surprised, therefore. God is omnipresent—there are no absences of God. God is impassible—divine being cannot receive effects. God is immutable—cannot change. God is all light—there is no darkness, no struggle, no shadow in God. God is perfect—there is nothing wanting in God's experience—God chooses to love us, but has no *need* of us.

Prior to the development of the Wisdom figure metaphor for God, the ancient Hebrew is concerned rather with the "who" of God, not in abstraction from human events, but in the midst of them. God is an historical actor. There is no wondering "what is God like apart from us?" The major characteristics are named psychologically rather than philosophically, and they are moral categories. The two that tower above all others are justice and mercy. Rigorous justice and tender mercy.

At one moment we confront the just anger of God. Yahweh says to Jeremiah: "Even if Moses and Samuel pleaded before me, I could not sympathize with this people! Drive them out of my sight; away with them! And if they ask you, 'Where shall we go?' tell them this, 'Yahweh says this: Those for the plague, to the plague; those for the sword, to the sword; those for famine, to famine; those for captivity, to captivity!' " (Jer 15:1–2). Before such anger, we begin to doubt that we can survive the anger of God. But almost as soon as we conclude that as sinners we cannot survive the justice of God we are touched by the incredible mercy of God, as Yahweh tells Jeremiah: "I shall be the God of all the families of Israel, they will be my people. . . . They have found pardon in the desert. . . . I have loved you with an everlasting love and so I still maintain my faithful love for you. . . . I shall forgive their guilt and never more call their sins to mind" (Jer 31 passim). It is almost as if God cannot decide whether it is finally justice or mercy that rules the divine heart.

The God of Jesus is not immutable, impassible, omnipotent, etc., but forever weaving back and forth between justice and mercy, keeping us guessing in the dialectic redemptive tension between them. In a "talents" parable about the Kingdom, the King pronounces against the person with one talent who hides it to keep it safe, because he heard the King is a hard man: "Any who has not will be deprived even of what he has. As for this good-for-nothing servant, throw him into the darkness outside, where there will be weeping and grinding of teeth" (Mt 25:14–30). In another parable about the Kingdom, a road bum is forced into the King's banquet feast for his son so that the celebration can bristle with people. However, the road bum is not wearing a wedding garment. The King tells the attendants: "Bind him hand and foot and throw him into the darkness outside, where there will be weeping and grinding of teeth" (Mt 22:1–14). In still another parable of the Kingdom, the Master deals with a servant whom he forgave a huge debt, but who in turn refused to forgive a small debt against him: "In his anger, the master handed him over to the torturers till he should pay all his debt. And that is how my heavenly Father will deal with you unless you each forgive your brother and sister from your heart" (Mt 18:23–35). If these are the only behaviors of God, most of us would be frightened most of the time.

However, this is the same God who will grant whatever a community asks in prayer (Mt 18:19–20). Or, if we, as evil as we are, would not give a stone to a hungry child who asks for bread, "how much more will your Father in heaven give good things to those who ask" (Mt 7:11). The mercy of God is especially visible in the teaching of Jesus in Luke. "There will be more rejoicing in heaven over one sinner repenting than over ninety-nine upright people who have no need of repentance" (Lk 15:7). The classic Lukan parable tells of a son who squanders his inheritance on debauchery (Lk 15:11–32). Ashamed and repentant, he begins rehearsing his confession to his father as he heads for home. But the father has no need of hearing the confession; it is enough that the son's face is turned once again toward the father. What the father does, in fact, is throw a magnificent party.

This tension between justice and mercy characterizes the God in the Earlier Scriptures as well as the teaching of Jesus in the Later Scriptures. And it continues to be thought out in the rabbinic materials. A Midrash presents God as deliberating whether to create the world out of justice alone (but then it could not endure) or out of mercy alone (then sin would abound).[50] So God creates it out of both, but does not tell us in what proportion. Just when we are about to relax in God's mercy, God's justice stands us on end. When we have almost resigned ourselves as sinners to the logic of God's justice, the logic of God's mercy rescues us. The impulse of Greek logic would be to find an explanation that provides coherence and clearly indicates the exact proportionality between the justice and mercy of God. For Jewish logic, it is exactly the non-logic that redeems: we must somehow live back and forth, for each is 100% the case; and it is precisely the ambiguity that keeps us on our toes and in right relation with God. Urbach cites an early Palestinian Sage:

> The Holy One, blessed be He, said to Moses: "What doest thou seek to know? *I am called according to My acts. Sometimes I am called El Shadday* ['Almighty God'], or *Shevaot* ['Hosts'], or *Elohim* ['God']; or *YHWH* ['Lord']. When I judge mankind I am called '*Elohim;* when I make war against the wicked I am called *Shevaot;* when I suspend man's sins I am called *El Shadday;* and when I have compassion on my world I am called *YHWH.*"[51]

God is named according to the ways that God is experienced in history, not in formal philosophical ways. This is not the timeless naming of the Greeks, but a thoroughly Hebrew, time-bound, historical naming. That was true of the naming of God in the Earlier Scriptures, and it is true of the renaming of God in the rabbinic period.

While Christians were naming God's omnipresence as a formal characteristic, the Sages devised some new names for God to describe their experience of God's presence: *Shekhina* and *Maqom*. *Shekhina* is related to the root verb meaning "dwell." In a text that comes from around the Bar Kokhba War, we read that if two people sit together to study the Torah, the *Shekhina* is there in their midst.[52] As the word develops, it names the closeness of God not merely to all of creation, but especially God's closeness to human beings. The meaning in respect to God, of course, is metaphorically grounded in the "dwell" meaning of the verb.

Likewise, *Maqom*, which literally means "place," comes to name the experience of God as near. And even though *Maqom* is often translated as "omnipresent," it does not carry that formal Greek sense. Rather, since the nearness of God is experienced any place one goes, "place" itself is a right designation. It is a very direct, clear, and unphilosophical name: God is just "place." "Place" is one of God's names.

Maqom, which names the nearness of God to all our places, is balanced with *Shamayim*, or "heaven." *Shamayim* and *Maqom* do not imply a two world view: natural earth and supernatural heaven. The meanings may be more analogous to immanence and transcendence (as long as transcendence does not mean "totally other"). Fundamentally, they name two truths of our experience: that God is both near and distant. Everytime I think I have hold of God in God's nearness, I am quickly reminded that God is always more than *Maqom*. Paul Tillich once talked about God beyond God. *Shamayim* is the "beyond," the "more than." *Shamayim*, the complement of *Maqom*, is the "grandeur" name that our experience of God requires (but not so grand as to constitute a metaphysical duality).

God's might is similarly named: *Gevura*. *Gevura* just means "power." Because the power of God is experienced in such abundance, the simple word "power" is a fitting name. Kings and generals may have power, but none so effectively and redemptively that the word "power" would be the people's name for them. *Gevura* and *Maqom* are illustrations of the dictum that "Less is more." Even though these words are often translated "omnipresent" and "almighty" or "omnipotent," the "al-" and "omni-" are imports. Better the Hebrew poetry of calling God just "Power" and just "Place." For that is so much!

Our Christian minds have for so long been schooled in God's immutability, impassibility, omnipresence, omnipotence, etc., that it is not easy to allow that Jesus had a substantially different sense of God. Our conversation with Jesus requires that we learn to hear with Jewish ears, or we risk not hearing him. And if we do hear him with Jewish ears, we also risk a creative transformation of some of the presuppositions about God that we brought with us into the start of the conversation. Serious, disciplined conversation with the Jewish Jesus-event on its own grounds will not leave all the settled instincts of our Christian inheritance intact.

God and Ambiguity

Finally (and it is the last point of this chapter), I want to show a contrast between the Greek and Hebrew constructions of God's meaning in respect to the pervasive reality of ambiguity. In a word, the Greek version tends to exclude ambiguity from deity; the Hebrew rendering does not (at least, not before the Wisdom figure evolves). To develop the "thick history" of this point, I will propose some examples from the Earlier Scriptures, the Christian Scriptures, the Midrash, and then add some contemporary reflections.

The Jewish Scriptures are not a unified production, and they do not offer a coherent, unified reading of history and God's activity. They are an immensely rich and varied collection of texts whose formation spans many centuries—they are classic texts that probe the heights and depths of religious experience. My reflections here are about one theme—a significant theme—that weaves in and out of those Scriptures.

While there is never the slightest temptation to affirm equality between God's power and human power, the Earlier Scriptures do regularly affirm *a genuine mutuality* between God and human beings. The Covenant could not operate without God's initiative in offering it, nor would it be redemptive without God's fidelity to it. But the Covenant is bi-partisan. It can only redeem human history when human beings are responsive to it. Human non-cooperation renders the Covenant impotent to redeem human life.

In his analysis of the contrasting Jewish and Christian narratives (or master stories) Michael Goldberg makes this point the central difference.[53] The Jewish Scriptures over and over again affirm that the power that redeems is mutual and relational (a point that Jesus will clearly make about the leaders he was forming). Goldberg comments that "this tale of the Lord's ongoing interaction with his people Israel offers sure evidence that history will ultimately work out . . . *only if God and human beings can mutually be relied upon to work things out together.*"[54] A relational power model places *real* limitation upon the power of each party to the mutual pact, and I believe that no theologic can bring consistency into this interpretation of God and the divine omnipotence of classical theism.[55] Real mutuality excludes unilateral control, and therefore absolute power.

It is not true, of course, that classical theism fails to affirm the importance of human cooperation with God—but the *importance* is never tantamount to a *redemptive necessity*. In classical theism there is no abiding sense that our lack of cooperation could effectively and permanently sidetrack the redemption God offers—delay it, perhaps, because God chooses to allow our freedom, but never finally to short-circuit it totally.

This issue is not thematically addressed in the synoptics, but I think it is safe to conclude that the God of Jesus Christ works mutually with us to effect the reign of God, for that is part of the assumptive world in which Jesus lives as a Galilean Jew. Michael Goldberg argues persuasively that the theme of God's unilateral saving power has some visibility in the passion narrative in Matthew. I do believe that a unilateral interpretation of redemption is beginning to make an appearance there. However, the community memory out of which the Matthean Gospel was spun did not belong to a Palestinian community—it was probably Antiochene, where some "bottom elephants" of the Greek mind would have been interpretively involved.

As I have already indicated, we must not too quickly attribute rabbinic materials written after 70 CE to Palestinian Jewish faith before 70. Yet it makes cultural sense to suppose some essential continuity. The Mishnah is a Palestinian document through and through. In its repudiation of Greek language and philosophy, it has more continuity with Palestinian Judaism than with nearly any of diaspora Judaism. I think it not untoward, therefore, to see the form and concerns of Mishnah, Tosefta, Midrash, etc., as evidence—not proof!—of deeply Hebraic cultural foundations for Palestinian Judaism in Jesus' time. Rabbinic Judaism simply does not go the Greek road. Therefore, time spent with basic rabbinic notions about God, world, human history, etc., will not tell us *exactly* how Jesus thought and felt, but they do give some assurance about the basic texture of the Jewish ethos in early first century Galilee. From Scripture to Mishnah the stories change and the written style changes; but the Yahweh of the Hebrew Scriptures and the Yahweh of the rabbinic documents are recognizably one and the same.

In the Earlier Scriptures, Yahweh struggles along with his people. Yahweh's people are sometimes petty, greedy, petulant, angry, lustful. Yet with all their creaturely foibles, they stay with God. To remain faithful to his promise, God too has come to terms with his own anger, his vindictive rage, and demanding jealousy. The Midrash, Slonimsky says, presumes that for God as well as human beings, historical processes occasion an enrichment and deepening of character.[56] The world is a growing, developing, struggling reality. It is incomplete, and with pain and sorrow finds its way. Slonimsky says that Midrash rejects the unpalatable conclusion that while God could prevent evil, he does not. Rather, God is afflicted along with the world, to which the following Midrashic account testifies:

> In the hour when God determined to destroy the Temple, he said, "So long as I am in its midst, the nations of the world will not touch it; but I will close my eyes so as not to see it and swear that I will not attach myself to it until

the time of the End (the Messianic era) arrives, then the enemy can come and destroy it" . . . Thereupon the enemy entered the Temple and burnt it. When it was burnt God said, "Now I have no dwelling place in the land; I will withdraw my Shekinah from it and ascend to my former place." In that hour God wept and said, "Woe is me, what have I done? I caused my Shekinah to descend for the sake of Israel, and now that they have sinned I have returned to my former place. Heaven forbid that I should become a laughing stock to the nations and a scorn to men." Then Metraton came and fell on his face and said, "Let me weep. But you must not weep." Then God said, "If you do not let me weep I will go to a place where you cannot enter and I will weep there, as it is said, 'My soul shall weep in secret places (Jr 13:17)'." Then God said to the angels of the service, "Come we will go, you and I, and see what the enemy has done to my house." So God and the angels of service set forth, Jeremiah leading the way. When God saw the Temple, he said, "Assuredly this is my house and my place of rest into which the enemy has come and worked his will." In that hour God wept. . . . Then God said to Jeremiah, "Go call Abraham, Isaac and Jacob and Moses from their graves, for they know how to weep. Then they all went weeping from one gate of the Temple to another, as a man whose dead lies before him."[57]

The enemy who destroyed the Temple is Roman might, but we cannot overlook the opening statement as well, that God decided to destroy the Temple. We seem to meet the shadow side of deity. Slonimsky says that the Midrash can afford "to tell the truth as we feel it with the sharp sting of reality: God is a very finite God in the world of actual things. We can say it if only we say it in the form of images which are not binding as sober formulated creed but which have the supreme value of tacit admission and irony."[58] Our primal grasp of the world is better told in metaphor than in categories of philosophical logic.

That there might be a divine darkness is not a possibility for the basic Greek symbols of deity. The image there is light—all light. God is only light, a theme strong in John's Gospel and in the Johannine letters. There is no ambiguity in classical theism, grounded as it is in Greek presuppositions.[59] Deutero Isaiah, however, knows there is only one God, and that one God must bear responsibility for the whole world. The whole world is always darkness and light, ambiguously good and ambiguously bad. To separate the good from the bad can only be done at the level of abstraction; in its concrete reality, the world is always both. And that world's God says:

I am Yahweh, and there is no other.
I form the light and I create darkness.

I make well-being, and I create disaster.
I, Yahweh, do all these things (Is 45:6b–7).

A Jew is told over and over to be holy as God is holy. If our image of the Ultimate Being is that of an absolutely unambiguous source of pure light and goodness, then we are condemned to disallow human darkness. Condemned is the right word, because to be a finite human creature is to have that darkness as well as light, and to have it irremediably. To construe meaning in that way is to construct a chasmic split in reality itself: an unambiguous God and a thoroughly ambiguous world.

Implied are two different presuppositions about moral goodness. For the Greek, perfect holiness means the total absence of evil impulses, of darkness. But, as I have indicated, in a significant tradition of Hebrew experience holiness consists rather in integrity: the ability to keep our loose ends together in love and fidelity.

Barbara Hannah, a Jungian psychologist, says that when we try to become what we cannot, flawless, a deep rift of guilt appears in our psyche—and has appeared in the Western psyche. Holiness, in the Hebrew mode, is more like wholeness in the Jungian mode: it means befriending the shadow, which still remains shadow and never surrenders its dialectical posture. Holiness, however, does not mean eliminating the shadow.[60] Although we are not accustomed, with our Greek ears, to take seriously these symbolic intuitions into the nature of ultimacy, they are there: notwithstanding God's jealousy and anger, and sometimes needing to be reminded of commitments by Abraham or by Moses, finally God is faithful. No matter what, God does not go away, even when staying means coming to terms with divine darkness. Fidelity to all our connectedness, based on love, is how this holiness is expressed. And that includes our fidelity to our own selves, shadow and all.

I have already indicated how the teaching of Jesus about the Reign of God continues to affirm a dialectic tension between the severity of God's justice and the tenderness of God's mercy. Recall also the advice of Jesus in the sermon on the mount. "Be perfect as your heavenly Father is perfect" (Mt 5:48). The Greek word for perfect is *teleios,* and it means "finished" or "flawless" or "with nothing lacking." This is probably a Greek rendering of an original Aramaic/Hebrew dictum, deep in the tradition: "Be holy as God is holy." The New Jerusalem Bible translation has what was surely Jesus' sense of the matter: "You must therefore set no bounds to your love, just as your heavenly Father sets none to his." The context of the preceding verses supports this translation of *teleios.*

We have seen that interpretation of the world, especially regarding issues

" . . . to be a finite human creature is to have that darkness as well as
light, and to have it irremediably."

of ultimate concern, projects out before us the possible stories our lives might tell. Thus, there is more than a semantic difference between trying to be holy by not having a sin to confess, or trying to be holy by not letting our sinful propensities put limits on our love. These are very different life tasks.

The Rabbinic tradition continues to develop many of these understandings—which I hold is evidence that these notions were probably hanging around in Palestinian Jewish intuitions in Jesus' time. The Sages speak about two inclinations that always dwell within us: the good inclination (*yetzer hatov*) and the evil one (*yetzer hara*).[61] God creates the *yetzer hara* as well as the *yetzer hatov,* and after examining the power of the dialectic between good and evil within us, R. Samuel bar Nachman finally dares to pass judgment on the evil inclination: "And, behold, it was very good!"[62] The ambiguous nature of sexual desire is sometimes cited as an example. Libido totally under control would not be libido, and without some lusty drive people would not marry and beget. To separate the evil inclination out from the good would be to destroy the very nature of sexual drive. Because the world itself is integrally made of both inclinations, Urbach notes that "the destruction of the evil inclination also implies the annihilation of this world," for the evil inclination is also "the inclination of life."[63]

There has been a traditional Christian response to these two laws, a response that I once espoused, but which now appears to me as destructive. It goes this way: God loves the sinner, but not the sin. Here is the problem. When I do good things, they are me, they are my life. When I sin, that too is me; my sin is my life. My sin is not something accidental that I do. My sin is me. I am an integral actor on the stage of life, and I love and I hate. I cannot be broken up into the sinner and the sin. God cannot love the whole me without loving everything, light and darkness, good and bad. If God cannot embrace my darkness, then I am treated as an abstraction. I am loved in abstraction from something that is indeed my life. Abstract love is not redeeming love, it is sundering love.

The Sages understood God to say, "My children, I have created for you the Evil Inclination, (but I have at the same time) created for you the Torah as an antidote. And as long as you preoccupy yourselves with Torah, he shall not have dominion over you."[64] It is worth recalling, as W. D. Davies has indicated, that Paul implies that Jesus Christ, as the new Wisdom, is also the new Torah.[65] Imagine how differently, then, soteriological interpretations of Jesus might have gone had they travelled, as rabbinic thought did, down the Jewish road. We might have said that Jesus is how Christians befriend their evil inclinations without neutering the essential passions of human life, nor capitulating to the *yetzer hara,* and that when this occurs, historical experience is redeemed.

Matthew Fox has countered the theology of original sin with a theology of original grace (original blessing).[66] The deliverances of experience about creaturehood suggest, rather, that original ambiguity is a closer description.

Reprise

In this chapter we have spent time with the history and the geography of Palestine in Jesus' time, and have looked most closely at Galilean Judaism in which he lived and moved and had his being. We cannot get inside the subjectivity of Jesus, of course. But if we accept, as I think we must, that our assumptive worlds are incubated in the womb of culture, then there are highly reasonable conjectures that we can make about Jesus' assumptive world. We must at least do our best at this, or we shall not hear the voice of the Jesus-event on its own grounds. We have had to walk through some thick history to get our Christian feet initially redirected toward the less travelled road.

I have tried to use Rabbinic sources judiciously, convinced of the continuity between the Pharisaic tradition in which Jesus lived and the great Rabbinic classics, Midrash, Mishnah, Tosefta, and the two Talmuds, though quite aware that we must not too quickly read their details back into pre-70 Judaism. The Maccabean revolt against Hellenization of the Jewish soul, the emergence of the Pharisees, the Zealot resistance to Romanization, the first Jewish war and the regrouping of the Pharisee/Rabbis at Yavneh (Jamnia), the Bar Kokhba revolt in 135 and the regrouping of the Pharisee/Rabbis at Usha in Galilee, and the formation of the Mishnah there in Galilee—these all seem such a profound commitment to protecting the integrity of the Jewish soul that I am led to conclude that Palestinian Judaism was indeed influenced by Greek culture, but that *the root metaphors of Judaism—the bottom elephants—maintained their basic Hebraic integrity.* This was especially true of Galilee. Seltzer observes that the survival of old habits of language was more common in the rural areas, and overt adaptation to Hellenic forms more prevalent in an urban environment.[67] Galilee was certainly countryside Palestinian Judaism. And except for Jerusalem, Judea too was rural. Yet even Jerusalem is never an urban environment like Alexandria or Antioch.

I have surely placed a lot of weight on the Hebraic option of post-70 Rabbinic Judaism as a clue to the Jewishness of Palestine. Post-70 Rabbinic Judaism did not walk a Greek road, even though that would have been easy and accommodating. This alone does not absolutely prove anything about Galilee in the time of Jesus. Yet it is at least highly indicative of the cultural tenacity of Jewish root metaphors in the little area of Palestine where Jesus lived and died. And I would still, of course, affirm a strong Hellenistic influence in Palestine, even a profound one—archaeological findings make that patently clear. But I think the Hellenistic impress upon Palestine never, finally, tinkered with soul.

We then saw some of the profound contrasts between the foundational metaphors of Greek and Jewish world-views, and how differently the same English word sounds, depending upon whether the ancestral voices that echo through the word are Jewish or Greek: God, holiness, perfection, sin, redemption, etc.

In the next chapter we shall continue our conversation with the Jewishness of Jesus by considering some types of Jewish figures that have been invoked in one way or another to engage in conversation with the Jesus-event, that is, to interpret the meaning of Jesus.

Notes

1. Thorlief Boman, *Hebrew Thought Compared with Greek* (Philadelphia: Westminster, 1960), p. 17.

2. German efforts to write history more scientifically generated a movement to recover a reliable historical portrait of Jesus. "The Aims of Jesus" of Hermann Samuel Reimaurus (c. 1760) was among the first of such efforts. In a remarkable piece of scholarship at the beginning of this century, Albert Schweitzer details the history of this *Quest for the Historical Jesus* (New York: Macmillan, 1964), and shows the unworkableness of its presuppositions.

3. The Gospels are not historical documents, but "rememberings" of particular communities. A real Jesus is remembered, but the memories are significantly shaped by the experience of the rememberers. This is evident in how different communities retell the same event, e.g., even such important events as the last supper and the resurrection.

4. Cf. James Robinson, *A New Quest for the Historical Jesus* (Naperville: Allenson, 1959). A good example of the new quest is Gunter Bornkamm's *Jesus of Nazareth* (New York: Harper, 1960).

5. Saul Lieberman, *Hellenism in Jewish Palestine* (New York: Jewish Theological Seminary, 1950). Victor Tcherikover, *Hellenistic Civilization and the Jews* (Philadelphia: Jewish Publication Society of America, 1959).

6. Martin Hengel, *Judaism and Christianity* (Philadelphia: Fortress, 1974); E.P. Sanders, *Paul and Palestinian Judaism* (Philadelphia: Fortress, 1983).

7. Eric M. Meyers and James F. Strange, *Archaeology: The Rabbis and Early Christianity* (Nashville: Abingdon, 1981), p. 78. The results of much recent archaeological explorations are yet to be published.

8. Geza Vermès, *Jesus the Jew* (Philadelphia: Fortress, 1981) and *Jesus and the World of Judaism* (Philadelphia: Fortress, 1983).

9. Sean Freyne, *Galilee from Alexander the Great to Hadrian 323 BCE to 135 CE* (Wilmington: Glazier, 1980).

10. Freyne, 1980, p. 29.

11. Freyne, 1980, p. 107.

12. Freyne, 1980, p. 112.

13. Freyne, 1980, pp. 114–121.

14. Freyne, 1980, p. 121.

15. Freyne, 1980, p. 124.

16. Freyne, 1980, p. 126.

17. Freyne, 1980, pp. 129, 131, citing Josephus.

18. Meyers and Strange, 1981, pp. 62ff.

19. This description of Galilean cities relies heavily on Meyers and Strange, 1981, pp. 56–58.

20. Meyers and Strange, 1981, p. 57.

21. Vermes, 1981, p. 49.

22. Meyers and Strange, 1981, p. 26.

23. Vermes, 1981, p. 44.

24. Vermes, 1981, p. 49.

25. Raymond E. Brown, *The Community of the Beloved Disciple* (New York: Paulist, 1979), pp. 35–36.

26. Raymond E. Brown and John P. Meyer, *Antioch and Rome* (New York: Paulist, 1983).

27. Vermes, 1981, p. 49.

28. This is the thesis of John B. Cobb, Jr., *Beyond Dialogue* (Philadelphia: Westminster, 1982).

29. Vermes, 1981, p. 47.

30. Freyne, 1980, p. 246.

31. E.g., Oscar Cullmann, *Jesus and the Revolutionaries* (New York: Harper & Row, 1970); and Martin Hengel, *Was Jesus a Revolutionist?* (Philadelphia: Fortress, 1971).

32. Marcel Simon, *Jewish Sects* (Philadelphia: Fortress, 1967), p. 45.

33. Freyne, 1980, p. 210.

34. Ellis Rivkin, *What Crucified Jesus* (Nashville: Abingdon, 1984). "And what is striking is that the Gospels confirm that no institution of Judaism had anything to do with the trial and crucifixion of Jesus" (p. 118).

35. Freyne, 1980, p. 221.

36. Rivkin, 1984, pp. 36–37.

37. Cf. Paul Ricoeur, *The Symbolism of Evil* (Boston: Beacon, 1969), "Conclusion: The Symbol Gives Rise to Thought," pp. 347–357.

38. George Foot Moore, *Judaism*, Vol. 1 (Cambridge: Harvard, 1927), p. 357.

39. Robert M. Seltzer, *Jewish People, Jewish Thought* (New York: Macmillan, 1980), p. 245.

40. Moore, 1927, p. 115.

41. Ephraim Urbach, *The Sages,* Vol. 1 (Jerusalem: Mignes, 1979), pp. 29–30.

42. Ricoeur, 1969, p. 348.

43. Boman, 1969, p. 205.

44. Boman, 1969, pp. 201–204.

45. Bernard Lee and Harry Cargas, *Religious Experience and Process Theology* (New York: Paulist, 1976), "The Appetite of God," pp. 369–384.

46. Abraham Heschel, *The Prophets,* Vol. 1 (New York: Harper & Row, 1962), p. 5.

47. Heschel, 1962 (1), p. 5.

48. Henry Slonimsky, *Essays* (Cincinnati: Hebrew Union College Press, 1967), p. 42.

49. Plato, *Laws,* VII, 803, cited in Heschel, 1962 (1), p. 5.

50. Moore, 1962 (1), p. 389.

51. Urbach, 1979 (1), p. 37.

52. Urbach, 1979 (1), p. 42.

53. Michael Goldberg, *Jews and Christians: Getting Our Stories Straight* (Nashville: Abingdon, 1985). I agree with Goldberg's assessment of the great contrast in the narrative structures of Judaism and Christianity vis-à-vis our relationship to God's activity. However, this only becomes a full-blown theme when Christian thought systematically embraces many of the presuppositions of the Greek world view.

54. Goldberg, 1985, p. 215, emphasis added.

55. I have developed this theme at greater length elsewhere. Cf. my essay, "Holocaust," in Harry James Cargas, editor, *When God and Man Failed* (New York: Macmillan, 1981), pp. 116–130.

56. Slonimsky, 1963, p. 32.

57. Slonimsky, 1963, pp. 42–43.

58. Slonimsky, 1963, p. 41.

59. I have dealt more fully with divine ambiguity in the chapter, "Long Night's Journey into Day," in William Dean and Larry E. Axel, eds., *The Size of God: The Theology of Bernard M. Loomer in Context* (Macon: Mercer Univ., 1987), pp. 63–76.

60. Barbara Hannah, *Encounters with the Soul* (Santa Monica: Sigo, 1981), pp. 246 ff.

61. Urbach, 1979 (1), pp. 471–483.

62. Urbach, 1979 (1), p. 424.

63. Urbach, 1979 (1), p. 475.

64. Urbach, 1979 (1), p. 472.

65. W.D. Davies, *Paul and Rabbinic Judaism* (Philadelphia: Fortress, 1980), pp. 147–176.

66. Matthew Fox, *Original Blessing* (Santa Fe: Bear & Co., 1983).

67. Seltzer, 1980, p. 195.

3
Jesus the Jew and Other Jews

Introduction: Religious Types

In this chapter, as Christians who have most often interpreted the meaning of Jesus by distinguishing him from other Jews, we will instead carry on a conversation with Jesus in his connectedness with other Jews. This is a road the Christian tradition has clearly not taken. I do not mean his relationships with particular Jewish women or men but with *kinds* of Jews that would have been familiar types to Jesus and his contemporaries. The list of types is a modest one: the Pharisee, the Teacher, the Wandering Charismatic, and the Eschatological Prophet.

As Christians, we must finally ask what it is that is particular to Jesus in which our own faith finds adequate mooring. But even when we interpret what is particular to Jesus, we do not have a full answer to the question: "Where do *we Christians* come from in our distinctiveness?" Only part of the answer is found in the particularity of Jesus. The other part is found in the historical and cultural conditions that accompanied and facilitated the evolution of Christian communities as entities outside of Judaism, events from about two generations' after Jesus. Those later events are crucial to questions about Christian identity, but they are not part of my inquiry in this book. I am anxious to explore Jesus' connectedness to his Jewish faith and culture as important to the interpretation of Christian meaning. This approach doesn't give a complete answer, but it tells a lot of truth.

Let us begin with the most historically complex of the types to consider: the Pharisee.

Pharisaic Origins

The continuum on which historians have located Jesus' relationship to the Pharisees is huge. On the one side, the Gospel polemics between Jesus and the Pharisees, especially in Matthew, and with the Jews more generally in John, led the Catholic Church in its Good Friday liturgy to speak about "the perfidious Jews." Rabbi Eleazer Slomovic, who kindly tutored me at the University of Judaism, told me that the most fearful day of the year for Jews in his

Eastern European country was Good Friday. After church services, some Christians would regularly rampage through the Jewish sections of the town. Jews would close their shops and hide out of fear. At the other end of the continuum is the recent book by Rabbi Harvey Falk, *Jesus the Pharisee.* Rabbi Falk contends that Jesus himself was a Pharisee, belonging to the House of Hillel.[1]

Who are the Pharisees? Where do they come from? What do they stand for? What are their religious, political and social functions in the time of Jesus? These are difficult questions. As Jacob Neusner has observed, the Pharisees just turn up in history, as it were, almost without a preparatory history; and when they make their first appearance, they are already a powerful presence in Jewish life.[2] There is preparation for them, of course, but not a well recorded one.

The theology of the Rabbis—successors to the Pharisees—is not written down until 200 CE and later. Nonetheless, these documents do incorporate some very early traditions that come from Pharisees in the time of Jesus.[3] But the historical reconstruction needed to judge and sort out these materials as sources for understanding the Pharisees is formidable. In my discussion I will rely heavily upon the more recent work of Jacob Neusner[4] and Ellis Rivkin.[5] All of these scholars are basically limited by the same three written sources: the Christian Scriptures (by which in this instance I include the Maccabees as well as the New Testament), the Jewish historian Josephus, and the rabbinic texts: Midrash, Mishnah, Tosefta, the Palestinian Talmud and the Babylonian Talmud. A few comments on each of these will be helpful.

For the most part, a very hostile attitude controls the way the Pharisees are presented in the Christian Scriptures. Ironically, notwithstanding all the criticism, the Gospels regularly show the Pharisees as the most influential Jewish sect in the time of Jesus, and their influence is not coercive. The people follow them willingly. And while Matthew's Gospel is regularly vicious, Luke is far more benevolent. In Luke's Gospel the Pharisees warn Jesus about Herod, and Pharisees also defend followers of Jesus in the post-Easter period. Some of them indeed even become Christians, Luke notes (Lk 15:5).

Christian and Jewish scholars alike recognize the unreliability of the Gospel presentation of the Pharisees. During the time of Jesus there are four major Jewish sects: Pharisees, Sadducees, Essenes and Zealots. However, at the time the Gospels are composed (after 70 CE), the Zealots have been crushed by the Romans; the Essene communities are destroyed; the Sadducees, oriented as they are to the Temple, no longer have a *raison d'être.* Only the Pharisees remain. During this period the Pharisees and the Christians are in contention for the soul of Judaism, and the animus between them is fierce. Much of the bitterness we feel in the Gospels is the anguish of the post-70 period read back into the historical life of Jesus.

Even through the polemic of Christian Scriptures, the influence of the Pharisees in the daily life of the Jews is clear. Rivkin notes that in the Gospels the Pharisees are never portrayed as separating themselves from the masses, and in their observances of the laws of ritual purity they are freely followed by the people at large. We do also hear accurately the historical concerns of the Pharisees: sabbath observance, ritual purity, dietary laws and tithing (which is related to dietary laws since tithed foods are made clean). Most important, the Gospels portray them as proponents of an Oral Law that goes beyond the Written Law.

The second important source is the historian Josephus. He was born c. 37 CE. He claims that he was himself a Pharisee. When the struggle against Rome began in 66, Josephus was sent to lead the Galileans. Perhaps a political realist, he served as an interpreter to the Romans during the siege of Jerusalem. Following the collapse of Jerusalem and the destruction of the Temple, he moved to Rome. He is the author of four works: *Antiquities,* an extensive history of the Jews, *The Jewish Wars,* dealing with more recent history, a treatise *Against Apion,* and the *Life,* an autobiography. He died sometime after 100 CE. Now one would think that being an historian, and himself a Pharisee, Josephus would provide a mine of trustworthy historical ore. But he has so many apologetic interests in his writing (an appeal not to blame Rome for the War, for example), that his remarks must regularly be evaluated and not always taken at face value. Sometimes in later work he says things at variance with earlier statements.

Even with these qualifications, Josephus remains one of the most important sources of information about the Pharisees. The political power of the Pharisees is once again clear in his work. Much of the detail that follows relies upon Josephus' work, especially as critically appropriated by Neusner and Rivkin.

The rabbinic materials are also a source of information. Recall that after the First Jewish War and the destruction of the Temple (70 CE), the leading Pharisees gather at Javneh (Jamnia) on the Mediterranean coast and there begin formulating Jewish life more explicitly, based especially upon the oral tradition. Then after the Second Jewish War (135 CE), this same work is continued at Usha, in Galilee. Completed in Galilee about 200, the Mishnah compiles under six major headings the details of the oral tradition. It contains sixty-two tractates. The authors are referred to as the Tannaim. About fifty years later a supplement is put together with similar materials not originally included in the Mishnah, which is the Tosefta. About 200 years after the Mishnah, the Palestinian Talmud is published. The Talmud is a further elaboration of the Mishnah. A Mishnah text will be accompanied by a commentary on it, a *Gemara.* The Palestinian Talmud contains about 750,000 words. A century later a Babylonian Talmud is published. This later set of commentaries on the Mishnah contains about 2,500,000 words. To these must also be added the Midrash, a looser collection of materials with stories and themes that often have a liturgical origin. The Rabbis or Sages who produced all of these (thus, the "rabbinic" materials) are usually considered direct descendants of the Pharisees.

The rabbinic sources contain much that deals with the Pharisees and their traditions, but they are written so long after the fact, and with such little self-conscious historical concern (in the modern sense), that it is difficult to disengage those materials that authentically speak about earlier history. For example, two of the most famous Pharisee Rabbis lived and taught in the period just before the adult life of Jesus: Hillel and Shammai. The rabbinic materials have detailed accounts of their teachings and their disputes. But Jacob Neusner persuasively concludes that these materials are later developments and barely if at all reflect the concrete lived experience of the two legendary Pharisees.[6] Neusner does a meticulously careful literary and historical/critical analysis of rabbinic texts, however, to isolate those materials which do give accurate information about the Pharisees. Ellis Rivkin handles these texts critically as well in his own reconstruction of the origins of the Pharisees, and does some sleuth work as an historical detective trying to establish the "plot" that underpins the evolution of the Pharisees.

There is no record of Pharisees before the Maccabean revolt. Rivkin concludes that this is clear evidence for their existence in 140 BCE. They seem to have emerged between 165 and 140, but about the specific details of these origins, we know nothing. The character of the Pharisees, however, becomes clear quickly once they appear on the scene.

The Pharisees are a lay movement of scholars. The name "Pharisees" comes from the Hebrew word *Perushim,* which means "the ones who are separate"—probably those set aside because they keep all the laws of ritual purity. Their separateness also expresses itself in *haveroth,* or "the table-fellowship of friends." It is not clear how tightly controlled this table fellowship is in the earlier history of the Pharisees. Neusner feels that *haveroth* is developed into a fairly exclusive fellowship sect by Hillel, and functions that way in the time of Jesus. This is helpful to know when we remember finding Jesus in table fellowship with the Pharisees. Tax collectors are specifically excluded from the Pharisees' table. The fact that Jesus eats with tax collectors would not be a live issue if Jesus were not being judged by the protocol of *haveroth*. This does not imply that Jesus was himself a Pharisee, but that he was considered by the Pharisees, in some fundamental ways at least, "one of us."

The Pharisees are also called by the Hebrew word *Hakhamim:* scholars or sages; and sometimes also *Soferim,* a word related to books and reading. *Sofer* is also translated as "scribe," which carries the meaning of learned people. They are scholars in the Law—that is, the Oral Law. And on this issue we are at the very heart of the identity of the Pharisees.

The Sadducees are the other mainstream sect of Jews in Jesus' time. They support the Temple and the priests. Sadducee seems related to the name *Zaddok,* the priestly family. The Sadducees are quite distinct from the Pharisees. They are a more conservative aristocracy. The Sadducees hold that only the written Law, or Torah, comes from Moses (the Pentateuch). They acknowledge the fact of tradition as well, but give it a very secondary place; for them the *only* normative source is the written Torah. They do not believe in resurrection, as do the Pharisees.

For the Pharisees the Oral Torah has the same normative force as the written Torah, and, in fact, sometimes supersedes the Written Torah. The Oral Torah is a guide to the everyday actions of religious Jews, setting down in detail the requirements of the sabbath, the ritual laws of purity, strict dietary laws, and regulations for tithing. These regulations are detailed and stringent, but the splendor of the Oral Tradition is missed if their *raison d'être* is passed over.

About the Hasmonean period, when the Pharisees arise, there are two factors that must be remembered: the secularization of religious institutions, and the need for accommodation to the powers-that-be if the Jewish people is to survive. First, under the Hasmoneans the Jews once again have a King. But the King is not from the House of David, where the messianic promise lies. The King does not carry the religious meaning of the Davidic House, nor is he self-consciously related to the Tribes of Israel. This is not to say that the Jews of the time are unhappy—they are delighted to be a nation once again. But they do not have the Messiah King, who must be Davidic. "Son of David" is, in fact, another way of naming the Messiah. Kingship as a religious institution has been secularized.

Secondly, the position of High Priest becomes a political plum rather than a religious function for a Zaddokite. Under the prescriptions of the Written Torah, the High Priest must be a member of the priestly family, but that succession has been interrupted. In Jesus' time the High Priest is a Roman appointee.

" . . . the protocol of *haveroth*."

The vestments of the High Priest are kept under lock and key by the Roman procurator. And only those High Priests who toe the line are kept in office (Caiaphas, the High Priest at the time of Jesus' trial, was in office longer than any other Roman appointee). Both King and Priest have lost their hereditary, religious meanings. The accommodations have Jewish survival at heart. The Pharisees enter the struggle to compromise without the loss of essential Jewish soul.

The Sadducees are a conservative party that tries to protect and foster the religious meaning of the Temple and the priesthood; they re-emphasize scripture alone as normative, a tilt in what we would today call a somewhat fundamentalist direction. Their membership is aristocratic. The response of the Sadducees to a tense social situation is traditionalism. The Pharisees, immensely popular with the masses of the people, fashion a different response to the same social situation.

The Pharisees attempt to relocate the Temple in the family by making the dietary and cleanliness rules of the Temple become rules of the home as well. Antagonistic readings of the Pharisaic movement see only the laws, and do not recognize that sanctification of the home and family is the underlying motive. These regulations are not originally intended so much to supplant the Temple altogether as to sanctify family and home life by making it a Temple as well. One of the reasons that Judaism is immediately able to continue even after its central symbol, the Temple in Jerusalem, is destroyed is that the sanctuary of family and home is already established as sacred space.

The relocation of some Temple-like sacred space, time and ritual within home and family reinterprets the meaning of the Jewish family. In so doing, it facilitates the continuation of Judaism over 1,900 years without a Temple or a sacred city. The relocation of ritual from Temple to home also makes the home an extraordinary context for identity formation. When we think of Pharisaism in the time of Jesus, we must keep remembering these remarkable contributions to Jewish existence, including the Jewish existence of Jesus.

The Pharisees are realists about a history of domination by others, and the cultural pressure upon Jews to compromise their religious and cultural identity. Neusner and Rivkin both acknowledge that the Pharisees are saying: "Exercise political control however you must, and we will cooperate so long as you make possible *our* power over the inner life of Israel."[7] When Jesus is asked about the lawfulness of paying Roman taxes, his response is deeply Pharisaic: "Give Caesar what is Caesar's and God what is God's." He doesn't fashion a new answer; he gives the Pharisees their own answer.

Although "liberal" is a modern word, I think the Pharisees, in the fundamental intuition that inspires them, must be seen as the liberal movement within the Judaism of its time. They not only recognize the socio-cultural needs for accommodation, they also affirm that God is acting through the changes and developments in norming ways. This can only mean that there must be an evolving Oral tradition that is no less norming than the Scriptures themselves. In this vein, Neusner writes:

> The concept of a truth outside of Scriptures opened the way to the accommodation of new ideas and values within the structures of inherited symbols. . . . The "oral Torah" opened the Judaic tradition to the future . . . thus preserving a welcoming attitude toward the world.[8]

The evolving Oral Torah is an interpretation of God's will in the present. I shall return again and again to this important notion of interpretation. A clear commitment to the role of interpretation in the continuing creation of Jewish identity is perhaps the most notable and remarkable characteristic—and achievement—of the Pharisees.

Pharisees: Torah, Halakhah

The Jewish word *Torah* is translated by the English word "Law," a not entirely but yet largely inaccurate rendering. It has more to do with "a guide for living," and includes multiple prescriptions. Let me cite an example. There is a rabbinic prescription that all people say one hundred blessings each day: "Blessed are you, Lord God of all creation, for . . . " There are blessings in morning and evening prayers (these alone cover fifty-four daily blessings), but also for the details of daily life: for rising, for the first toilet of the day, the first food of the day, etc. I recall a lecture in which a Christian theologian cited the one hundred blessings as an example of the legal burden of minute prescriptions to which the Rabbis/Pharisees bound every Jew. But I also remember a class lecture by a rabbi who explained that God is blessed each time something pleasureful, useful or lovely is experienced, and the message of the one hundred blessings is permission to enjoy the world. The blessings are a ritual affirmation of the world, the body, meals, etc. As in any tradition, practices that make immediate good sense in their origins often get encrusted in a tradition that then blocks access to the original cause or inspiration. We ourselves construct directives for a reason we understand. Then we often obscure the fact that we constructed the directives, because in so doing we hide their relativity and thus make them more binding ("it came from God," or "that's simply the way the world is"). Sometimes this is the case with the Oral Tradition.

The Pharisaic "law" comes to be known as *Halakhah*. I would like to cite Neusner on the Jewish sense of this word:

> [Halakhah] is normally translated as "law," for the *halakhah* is full of normative rules about what one must do and refrain from doing in every situation of life and at every moment of the day. But *halakhah* derives from the root *halakh*, which means "go," and a better translation would be "way." The *halakhah* is "the way": *The way* man lives his life; *the way* man shapes his daily routine into a pattern of sanctity; *the way* man follows the revelation of the Torah and attains redemption. For the Jewish tradition, this "way" is absolutely central.[9]

In this context, we must recall that the earliest known name for Christians was "the Way." Paul persecutes those "of the Way" (Acts 9:25). When Paul preaches Jesus Christ in the synagogue, some of those who disagree attack "the Way" (Acts 19:9). The presence of "the Way" in Ephesus causes riots (Acts 19:23). When Paul defends himself before Felix, he says that he preaches "the Way," even though some people consider "the Way" just another sect [within Judaism] (Acts 24:14). And Luke adds that Felix himself was well informed about "the Way" (Acts 24:22).

Inasmuch as Paul himself is a Pharisee, as are some of the early Christians, I think we should not rule out a feeling of genetic connection between the Jesus "Way" and the *Halakhah* "Way." It is certainly the case that Paul and these early communities do not think of their Christian commitment as being outside of Judaism, or alongside it. The intimation that Jesus might be a continuation of Oral Torah suggests a feeling of continuity rather than discontinuity. I am not suggesting that Jews could or should accept Jesus as a new development of *Halakhah*. But that might be a Christian way of interpreting Jesus, first of all acknowledging the beauty of *Halakhah*, and secondly remembering better Jesus' Jewishness.

In support of such a connection between Jesus and the motif of Oral Law, we need also recall that Jesus taught and argued much as the Pharisees did. Jesus characteristically taught in parables. As Michael Cook has pointed out, rabbinic literature has parables about: a king who hires laborers who in turn complain about the distribution of wages; a king who gives a banquet which invited guests fail to attend; a father who lovingly accepts a wayward son who returns penitently; lost coins and treasure, etc.[10]

Like the Rabbis and probably the Pharisees, Jesus used the Scriptures for "proof texting," that is, taking a verse out of its original context and applying it to some immediate issues (a technique also favored by Matthew). Jesus did not write. As a teacher he taught in the mode of an oral tradition.

My point is not the validity of *identifying* Jesus with *Halakhah,* but rather of using *Halakhah* as a metaphor for interpreting the meaning of Jesus. Recall that a metaphor is based upon some genuine likeness shared by two entities. And in this case, the likeness is grounded in an historical situation in which Jesus and the Pharisees live. The fact that Jesus is not simply identified as a Pharisee also means that some un-likeness haunts the metaphor. Had Jesus formally been a Pharisee, I do not see how this could have escaped the early records so totally. But deep resonances between the proclamation of Jesus and the teaching of the Pharisees must be acknowledged.

When Davies suggests the possibility of a New Torah christology, his reasons are different from those which I proposed. He follows Paul in making a connection with Wisdom. His "is like" resemblance is based upon the equation of the Wisdom figure with Torah in the Jewish tradition and Paul's Wisdom interpretation of Jesus.[11]

As I have indicated already, and shall treat more extensively later, the developed Wisdom figure probably lies outside the assumptive world of Galilean Judaism in Jesus' time. That doesn't make the metaphor wrong, but it does mean that we are no longer interpreting the voice of Jesus with images taken from the assumptive world of Jesus. My suggestion is that "the Way" is a very early name for Christians, and therefore a very early christological interpretation of Jesus. I am also suggesting the reasonable possibility that "the Way" suggested itself to people who were familiar with "the Halakhah" in the Rabbinic/Pharisaic sense of the word. If so, there was a felt connection. While we can't posit with assurance the contents of someone's mind on the matter long ago, we can at least say that *Halakhah*/Way is a christological resource that is worth reclaiming today: it has the virtue of doing no violence to the Jewishness of Jesus while at the same time connecting with a very early interpretation of Christian life.

Pharisees: Piety and Politics

What first gains for the Pharisees the explicit attention of Josephus is their political importance. As Neusner phrases it, between that time and Jesus' time, they move from politics to piety. But then after 70 CE they assume political importance again. Before addressing some of that history, I want to recall a point made in the previous chapter which has importance here.

While the Jews clearly distinguished the majesty and power of God from any human strength, this was nonetheless a God known always and only through historical events. The Covenant included God's transformation of history. God and the world are not separated metaphysically. The distinction between temporal and non-temporal was not instinctively Jewish. Therefore, the distinction between politics and religion must not bear the weight of the later ontological distinction between secular and sacred, or natural and supernatural. For the ancient Jew, moving back and forth between politics and piety is largely a matter of emphasis, of responsiveness to the needs of the Jewish spirit at some particular moment in history.

Clearly, the first unmistakable appearance of the Pharisees is in the context of their political significance. Alexander Jannaeus, who reigns from 104–76 BCE, is at first a follower of the Pharisees, but later alienates them deeply as he takes up with the Sadducees. He alienates the populace as well by his cruelty. Before he dies he advises his wife, Salome Alexandra, to court the Pharisees and thus re-establish a safe power base for herself and continuity for the family dynasty. It is good advice, and it works. In his history of these times, Josephus describes the Pharisees as a body of Jews with the reputation of excelling the rest of their nation by their observances of religion, and as exact exponents of the law. With the support of Salome Alexandra, the Pharisees are fierce in their retaliation, however, and proceed to kill whomever they wish.[12]

Rivkin locates an effective Pharisaic presence even earlier, at the installation of Simon Maccabee as high priest in 140 BCE. The crucial text is 1 Maccabees 14:25–48. The high priesthood, according to the Written Torah, traces its lineage through Aaron, Eleazar, Phinehas, and Zadok. A Great Synagogue (*Knesset ha-Gedolah*), i.e., a Large Assembly, of priests and people, princes and elders, made Simon both high priest and ethnarch, both the religious and the political leader. Rivkin notes something quite extraordinary in this Great Synagogue meeting. High Priesthood is transferred from the Zaddokite line to the Hasmonean line, contrary to the Written Law. The Great Synagogue, which is legitimated nowhere in the Scriptures, is higher in authority than priests or the received Torah. Rivkin concludes that there must already be a two-fold law operative at this time, which he understands to be that of the Pharisees.

The political power of the Pharisees is very significant in both of the incidents noted; but even though the political aspect is in focus, it is rooted in the acts of religious interpretation in which the Pharisees engage. We are reminded once again that in every act of interpretation there is some element of free construction—and what is remarkable about the Pharisees is that the free construction is a self-conscious activity. Interpretation is out in the open. From our perspective today we would recognize that the Sadducees as well could not but interpret as they adhered to the Written Torah. The Pharisees, however, *deliberately* reinterpret the meaning and requirements of Jewish life.

In Jesus' time the leadership of the Pharisees is principally in the area of piety, and not politics. All the reported disagreements between Jesus and the Pharisees have to do with elements of *Halakhah,* regulations for daily life in the areas of ritual and dietary observances. Again, we cannot always tell when the purported disagreements are read back from later history, and when they reflect actual historical disagreements. But even in the latter case, the disagreements are not sufficient to interrupt the possibility of Jesus' presence at the table fellowship of the Pharisees.

If the power of the Pharisees over the religious life of the Jews is emphasized in Jesus' time (their role in piety), we must still remember that the freedom which the Pharisees have over religious life is the basis of compromise that allows the Romans to rule. The Romans rule with the complicity of the High Priest whose non-Pentateuchal legitimation is part of the "hidden revolution" of the Pharisees. The difference between politics and piety is never finely drawn.

After both wars with the Romans, the Pharisees regroup and are given political power over Jewish life. But these are also the times when the great religious documents of a new Judaism are brought together by the Rabbis, the progeny of the Pharisees. From their first appearance, then, the Pharisees are a group to be reckoned with. They are very influential, and their theater of influence fluctuates between politics and piety, but always touching both.

Pharisees and the Influence of the Greek Academy

Insofar as the emergence of the Pharisees occurs during a period of great Hellenistic presence, the question of Greek influence is inevitable. The Pharisees are a kind of academy of scholars who relate careful learning to holiness and happiness. A gathering such as the *Synagogue Megale* described above has a clear resemblance to the gatherings of Greeks in the democratic polis to make decisions—a resemblance which the Hebrew name *Knesset ha-Gedolah* does not veil. Bickerman claims that the notion of an intelligentsia separate from clergy and sanctuary is surely a Greek inspiration.[13] I agree with that, and want to affirm some *formal* resemblances. But I also want to insist on how fundamentally different are the *material* concerns of the Greek scholars and the Jewish Sages.

The speculative Greek mind is concerned with individual ideas, and with systems of ideas and their internal logic. There is a sense that the contemplation of truth is the final achievement of human satisfaction. But the Sages are concerned with behaviors and their relationship to human fulfillment. The behaviors themselves are not the goal, but rather the internalization of their meaning in the orientation of life. If we want to see how Greek ideas enter into the construction of Jewish meaning, Philo is the place to go. Yet the difference between any tract of Philo and any tract from Mishnah makes clear how deeply Jewish are the concerns of the *Hakhamim*/Pharisees. If the inspiration for some kind of academy of scholars is Greek, Greekness does not impinge noticeably upon the content of the scholarly concern of the Pharisees. In the Pharisaic and Rabbinic tradition, there is no consorting with Greek root metaphors!

The Pharisees on the Individual

Ellis Rivkin's reconstruction of Pharisaic origins in *The Hidden Revolution* is subtitled *The Pharisees' Search for the Kingdom Within*. The final chapter in the book is called "God So Loved the Individual." This is a theme that deserves our attention as we ponder Jesus' relation to the Pharisees, especially in the context of what he might have learned from them. This concern for exploring the meaning of individuality is a far wider phenomenon than the Pharisaic influence in Palestine, but the wider event is also the latter's context.

In his very influential work, *The Origin and Goal of History,* Karl Jaspers traces the emergence of self-conscious human individuality as a far-ranging phenomenon in human history between 800 BCE and 200 BCE.[14] He calls this the axial period. I will take this theme up again in volume II, in a discussion of Israel's experience of "corporate personality." But some attention to this theme will be in order now to deepen our understanding of the Pharisees, especially in the context of attending seriously to responsible individuality.

Jaspers shows the development of the individual in China, India, Iran, Palestine and Greece:

> What is new about this age . . . is that man becomes conscious of Being as a whole, of himself and his limitations. He experiences the terror of the world and his own powerlessness. He asks radical questions. Face to face with the void he strives for liberation and redemption. By consciously recognising his limits he sets himself the highest goals. *He experiences absoluteness in the depths of selfhood and in the lucidity of transcendence.* . . . He becomes uncertain of himself and thereby open to new and boundless possibilities. . . . These paths [multiple cultural ways of being a human individual] are widely divergent in their conviction and dogma, but common to all of them is man's reaching out beyond himself by growing aware of himself within the whole of Being and the fact that he can tread [the paths] only as an individual on his own.[15]

Psychologists today sometimes speak of the psychological birth of an infant, meaning that only through time does a child become aware of her/himself as an entity separate from the womb and breast and arms of mother; and only after separateness is established does the social reality of interdependence come back into strong, active play. Analogously, the human race comes to this awareness of individuality somewhere in time also—in what Jaspers calls the axial period. The working out of individualness is a long, long affair.

As Jaspers indicates, not all cultures respond in the same way to the dawning awareness of human individuality. The Greek response includes an emphasis upon individuals as autonomous selves, and great reliance upon the truth of individual reason. The Jewish response on the part of the prophets, which is the Palestinian axial development, is more basically moral than rational. Personal responsibility is stressed.

Rivkin compares the Graeco-Roman and Jewish sense of individual. For the Greek and the Roman, law is external, and applies so long as one is in the political situation, the *politeuma,* where the constitution is in force. But the Jewish law binds Jewish individuals wherever they may be. The followers of the Pharisees carry with them wherever they are an internalized *politeuma.* ''Whereas for the Greeks and Romans this constitution encircled the individual, binding them from without, the *politeuma* of the Scribes-Pharisees was encircled by the individual and bound him from within.''[16] In so doing, the Pharisees deepen an appropriation of individuality that was initiated in Judaism by the prophets.

The stress upon the individual responsibility of the heart is a very old one in Jewish faith. It is reflected already in Deuteronomy, though dating this text is not easy (we are clearer about the written form than about its oral origins): ''Yahweh your God will circumcise your heart and the heart of your descendants, so that you will love Yahweh your God with all your heart and soul, and so will live'' (Dt 30:6). Not only must the flesh of the male be circumcised, but so too must the hearts of all Jews be circumcised. The Law must be an inside responsibility, not an outside imposition. The prophets reappropriate this very Jewish intuition, and develop it into a stronger but very Jewish sense of individual human being.

Jeremiah is a good example of this internalizing, subjectivizing reinterpretation of human existence. He takes the deuteronomic decision—circumcision of the heart—and develops further the notion of the inner responsibility of the individual subject. The terms of Covenant were originally on tablets of stone. Jeremiah interprets Yahweh as saying that now the Law is written on hearts (Jr 31:33). There will not be just the written commandment to worship God, but Yahweh will now be putting the impulse to respect God within the heart (Jr 32:40). The center of direction is within.

The Pharisees continue on this trajectory, as they give interpretation a very large role in further internalizing and individualizing personal existence for the Jews. For example, locating the holiness of the Temple within home and family is a deepening of personal religious responsibility. That internalization is the intention at the base of the Oral Law, a most important point that Christian commentators have regularly and tragically missed.

Not because they are Pharisees but because they are human beings, undoubtedly the Pharisees sometimes lose their orientation toward the kingdom within, and do just the opposite: they put the law around the individual on the outside. It should not be difficult for Christians to understand this; an example from Roman Catholic history might help. Abstaining from meat on Friday was originally intended to help Catholics internalize the meaning of Good Friday; but it became an external law binding under pain of serious sin.

Recall that Jesus says he has no intention of abolishing either the Prophets or the Law. He then criticizes the Pharisees for their preoccupation with external details, and gives a long discourse on the need to internalize the directives of the Law and the Prophets (Mt 5:17–48): "You have heard how it was said to our ancestors, *You shall not kill.* But I say this to you, anyone who is angry with a brother or sister will answer for it before the court. . . . You have heard how it was said, *You shall not commit adultery.* But I say this to you, if anyone looks at another lustfully, that person has already commited adultery in the heart." If this was an historical criticism of the behavior of *some* of the Pharisees on the part of Jesus, the very important point to note is that the criticism is made from a principle internal to Pharisaism itself about the movement within the heart that is proper to *individual* Jews.

The notion of individual repentance, which is proposed clearly in the prophets (esp. Ezekiel) and then developed in the Rabbinic/Pharisaic tradition is, as Moore notes, the great religious significance of repentance: "It not only became a cardinal doctrine of Judaism—its doctrine of salvation—but it impressed upon the religion itself its most distinctive character."[17] And nowhere, Moore writes, is the individualizing of religious responsibility more conspicuous than in the Jewish interpretation of a universal judgment where each is judged on the basis of personal conduct.[18] In the Jewish deep story, the moral individual exists in a radically social context. After a discussion of responsibility in cases of murder, the Mishnah recalls that God indicts Cain for spilling his brother's *bloods.* Because *bloods* is plural, the Mishnah concludes that not only the blood of Abel but of his progeny as well cries out from the ground. Then it continues:

For this reason man was created a singular individual: to teach you that anyone who destroys a single soul of human kin, Scripture reckons him as having destroyed the entire world. [Contrariwise] whoever preserves alive a single soul of humankind, Scripture reckons him as having preserved alive the entire world. [These verses are also meant] to tell us of the greatness of the Holy One praised be He. For when a human mints many coins with a single seal, all of them are identical with each other. But when the King of Kings, the Holy One, blessed be He, stamps every individual with the seal of the first man, no one individual is identical with another. Therefore, every individual is required to say, "Because of me the world was created." (TBSan 5:1)[19]

Needless to say, Jesus' own discourse on universal judgment expresses both individual responsibility (each good person is rewarded for good deeds, each evil person is punished for evil deeds), and also universal human connectedness (when you did it for anyone, you did it for me).

A similar point can be made about sabbath observance. If a sick person who can be relieved of infirmity is not cured because it is the sabbath, then the sabbath does not serve human life. As Lauterbach points out, the teaching of Jesus that the sabbath is made for human beings and not the reverse is good Pharisaic doctrine (cf. Mekilta Shabbata I).[20] Again, if any of these interactions with the Pharisees do come from the mouth of Jesus, it is a Jesus who is speaking from Pharisaic principles. Especially as these texts occur in Matthew, we must always keep in mind that in this Gospel Jesus clearly holds that the Pharisees do sit in the chair of Moses, that is, their teaching is authentic. The problem is that the details (which are to be followed, Jesus says) become such a preoccupation that people lose sight of weightier matters.

If Jesus were not offering some of his criticism from principles internal to Pharisaism, and if all the terrible polemic against the Pharisees (esp. in Matthew) and against the Jews generally (esp. in John) were historical, it would be difficult to understand Jesus' presence at Pharasaic *haveroth* or the accounts of the Pharisees addressing Jesus as Master or Teacher. But there he is in table fellowship with them. If there is conflict (as I think is the case over sabbath and over dietary practices), the conflict is not larger than the solidarity which seems to obtain in spite of it. For the Pharisees are, after all, in the words of Rivkin, "the grand internalizers."[21] Perhaps just because internalization is their intention, failures to do so seem all the more culpable when they do occur.

Belief in afterlife is another development that affirms individual worth. One of the clearest distinguishing marks between the Pharisees and the Sadducees is that the Pharisees believe in the resurrection of the body, which Rivkin and others see as part of the Pharisees' sense of the worth of each individual to God. Belief in resurrection is, therefore, a quite late development in Judaism. Jesus' own teaching about resurrection clearly locates him with the Pharisees. He is not teaching anything new. Even Paul seems to suggest that the "proof" of the resurrection is not so much that resurrection is a stupendous miracle that sets Jesus off from all others, but that since only the good are returned to God as individuals in the resurrection, the resurrection is effectively God's approval of Jesus.

Pharisees—The Grand Interpreters

In my last consideration of the character of the Pharisees, I return directly to the empiricist/historicist/hermeneutic concerns I named in the first chapter. All knowledge begins somewhere in lived experience. There is no knowledge of God that does not begin somewhere in our historical experience, and no theological understanding that is not at the same time an historical understanding. Not only is the experience of God historically conditioned, it is also only and always interpreted experience. While events themselves truly shape our "facts," so does our interpretation help constitute what we name "facts." In some measure, the interpreter always gets into the "facts." Events, combined with our active interpretation of them, together constitute what we call the facts, even the fact of God-in-our-experience. The originative or causative event and its interpretation can never be securely separated out to leave some kind of pure event-fact. To adapt Cornel West's historicist description of philosophy, I would understand that transient social practices and contingent cultural descriptions are also the proper subject matter for theology.[22] That is the nature of history, and thus of religious history as well.

The imprint of history and culture from a very particular time is evident in the behavioral prescriptions of Deuteronomy, Leviticus and Numbers. Certainly, when these materials from earlier history were codified and written down after the exile, they were handled selectively because they were intended for identity formation in a quite new context. Whenever in post-exilic time they are read in Hebrew, they are respoken immediately in Aramaic—not an attempt at literal translation, but an interpretative rendering. Even, therefore, when the tradition has been committed to writing, the need for ongoing interpretation is clear:

> In full view of all the people—since he stood higher than them all—Ezra opened the book. . . . And Jeshua, Bani, Sherebiah, Jamin, Akkub, Shabbethai, Hodiah, Maaseiah, Kelita, Azariah, Jozabab, Hanan, Pelaiah, who

were Levites, explained the Law to the people, while all the people kept their places. Ezra read from the book of the Law of God, translating and giving the sense; so the reading was understood (Ezr 8:5–8).

A continuing transformation of the Law of religious life is endemic to Jewish life. The Covenant itself underwent successive transformations, from Noah's rainbow to its "heart-felt" relocation in Jeremiah. Earlier still, the movement from governance by judges to rule by a king was a response to the socio-political situation of Palestine at that time. And this required some reinterpretation of the Covenant. When the Pharisees, therefore, become far more articulate about their interpretative development of an Oral Law, they are making explicit what has long been implicit.

The Pharisees do not only interpret and reinterpret (which in each instance involves some free reconstruction); they also generate new practices. Rivkin believes that the authority of the Great Synagogue which made a Hasmonean into a high priest is such an instance. Although the language comes from a later time in the Pharisaic/Rabbinic tradition, there is a clear acknowledgment that *Halakhah* is a free construction of new normative guidance: "We do not deduce the words of the Torah from the Words of the Soferim [Sages]; nor the words of the Soferim from the words of the Torah; nor the words of the Soferim from the words of the Soferim."[23]

That Jesus should teach new things and speak with authority is not a rare phenomenon in his time. Some people question his authority; but others simply marvel at it. That Jesus is experienced at speaking with authority is well nigh historically certain. But that Jesus should teach with such immediacy, though stunning, is not as unique as the new quest for the historical Jesus sometimes wanted to affirm. The Hebrew tradition is always open to redevelopment, through responsive interaction with new social situations and through new religious experience. It is clearly in the spirit of Jesus—in the Pharasaic spirit of Jesus, that is—to make the same claim for Christian existence. Because history is on the move, no particular historical experience of God can adequately address all other historical situations without insistent reinterpretation.

For the insights into the Pharisees which follow, I am much indebted to William Dean's historicist analysis of Hebrew Law, and to the work of Derrida on this topic to which Dean has called my attention. Dean compares the Hebrew and American traditions of law. Neither derives law from transhistorical ordering or eternal logos, but from historical experience. The United States court systems, from the lowest to the highest, depend upon normative guidance from written laws, from precedents (particular applications of the law), and from ongoing reinterpretations of precedents. Like the Pharisees, we find nor-

mative guidance in both the written tradition and the oral tradition. Americans
are like

> . . . Hebrews in their efforts to found themselves on historical actions rather
> than on transhistorical ideals. Americans, like Hebrews, are a nation of wan-
> dering emigrants who continue to reinterpret their covenant with God as they
> restlessly cross space and time, and who, in that series of reinterpretations,
> create their religious reality. . . . [They] create their religious truth from
> actions—present actions reinterpreting earlier actions, thereby becoming
> new actions, over and over again.[24]

This understanding must not be taken in a simplistic subjectivist way. The Jewish tradition has always affirmed the objective activity of God in history. But
along with this affirmation goes the presupposition that God too is historical
in the fullest sense. The experience of God which generates and norms religious behaviors, therefore, is never understood as the experience of a transhistorical, eternal ordering, but as historically conditioned and humanly
interpreted interaction between God and human beings. It is humbling to recognize and acknowledge our construction in what we know as revelation, including Jesus' construction in the disclosure of God in him.

John Pawlikowski is certainly correct when he argues that "the Pharisaic
revolution, leaning into the ministry and self-consciousness of Jesus, constituted [a] . . . monumental drift in human history."[25] A fundamental transformation of human self-understanding is afoot. The axial movement, begun in
Palestine among the prophets, is developed decisively into a modern form by
the Pharisees. Individuality is achieved under the auspices of profound moral
choices lived out among historical ideals, in contrast with the Greek emphasis
upon rational, speculative operations of the mind, and transhistorical ideals.
For Jesus, our individuality is radically socialized by God's Parent/Father/
hood, the moral consequences of which are a transformation of all the relational webs of human life into the Reign of God on earth. (I shall return to this
at length in the christology of volume three.)

In the work cited earlier, Dean indicates what I take to be another dimension of the "monumental drift in human history" which Pharisaism pro-
motes. Derrida uses "speaking" to refer to the immediate, unreflective talking
which people do together, and "writing" or "literality" to refer to any form
of writing or talking in which people are dealing reflectively with the past, that
is, deliberately reinterpreting history for the meaning it yields for living. Thus,
some forms of talking, when reflective interpretation is occurring, would be
in the category of "writing" for Derrida. Derrida (a Sephardic Jew) claims

that in Judaism lies "the birth and passion for writing," and the "radical origin of literality."[26] In the garden, Adam and Eve were "speaking" with God. With exile from the garden, "speaking" ends and "writing" begins. Derrida understands the Pharisees to have developed the "literality" of Jewish religious experience to new heights. In Derrida's categories, the Oral Law of the Pharisees is really in the category of "writing." The great Rabbinic documents are also its written form in the more traditional sense of "writing."

I must jump ahead into the content of the second volume of this work to say what difference all of this makes to how Jesus' voice is to be understood by us today. In the *logos* christology of John's Gospel, Jesus' conversation with God is almost like Adam's and Eve's "speaking" with God in the garden before their sin. Jesus' familiarity with God is a kind of "speaking" (Jn 17), a direct talking that has its foundation in Jesus' pre-existence with God as *logos*/Word. *Logos* is a Greek way of understanding reality that John makes use of to interpret Jesus. *Logos* is the eternal ordering, for all things, that is in God, and Jesus is the incarnation of that *logos* in history. In its essence, the *logos* is transhistorical.

Now a *logos* understanding of reality would surely not have been part of the assumptive world of Jesus himself. I am not arguing about its validity as a cultural appropriation of Jesus as a Christ-event. But I am saying that it is, in Derrida's terms, a form of writing which in effect locates ultimate value in transhistorical reality. This interpretation of Jesus turns our heads away from history, a singularly un-Jewish nod.

Jesus' speaking with God in John is analogous to Moses' speaking with God in Exodus. They are later interpretations of the meaning, respectively, of Christian existence and Jewish existence. The talking of Moses and Jesus belongs to Derrida's category of "writing." But *logos* "writing" belongs to a tradition that makes of God a transhistorical, "totally other" kind of reality, and derives the ordering of history from an eternal *logos*. The cosmic christology of Colossians is also such an interpretation (probably based on Wisdom).

If there is a cosmology in Derrida, it goes this way: all there is, is "writing," and our writing is what organizes and orders history. It is the great discovery of the Pharisees to get grounded in this literality, and elevate relentless interpretation to the status of sole historical norm. And for a Jew, of course, God is a primary historical actor, so that the mutuality of God and us is precisely what we relentlessly interpret.

If it is accurate to affirm, as I am doing, a very close genetic connection between Jesus and the Pharisees, then Jesus must be heard as speaking squarely out of their (and his!) tradition, i.e., as remaking religious identity in new sit-

uations, "not from beyond history, but only from historical events and interpretations in their own previous lives, events and interpretations which they
continually reinterpreted to meet new needs."[27]

This may seem a belabored point. But the Christian tradition has so
stressed the contrast between Jesus and the Pharisees that his continuity with
them is hardly visible. We easily miss Jesus' own interpretive role in the social
construction of the Reign of God right here in human history.

Jesus does continue to reinterpret the tradition he received, but in its own
direction. The sabbath laws forbade carrying objects anywhere outside the
home. The Pharisaic/Rabbinic tradition made provision for people living near
each other to co-own a central alleyway and thus allow one person to place
something in the common area so that a co-owner can then take the needed
object to another house. Though the details of this operation are legally intri-
cate, their purpose is to reinterpret sabbath law to make it easier to meet human
needs. When Jesus challenges the sabbath laws, the intention is to respond to
human need. The point here is that Jesus' own life is a testimony to the normative role of on-going interpretation.

This Pharisaic understanding of the historical origins of religious norms
contrasts fundamentally with the Greek *logos* interpretation of the same phenomenon. If religious behaviors are simply the logic of an eternal order, then
the religious task is deductive in nature: plotting the consequences of the eternal ordering in a given historical circumstance. Such law is not historicized,
only its applications. As Dean says, "it offers to the citizen some way out of
the chaos of history. The law stands in history but points beyond history. People of the [eternal] law are not creatures of history, but pilgrims through history."[28] The modern Western critique of religion (Feuerbach, Nietzsche,
Freud, etc.) rightly observes that temporal pilgrims on the way to non-temporal
happiness are not inclined to take *this* history with full seriousness.

Interpretation, on the other hand, is more inductive in nature. It makes
new judgments based upon new circumstances, and recognizes these judgments as normative interpretations of God's immediate presence. What is normative is not primarily the content of the law (though indeed some laws in the
Judaeo-Christian tradition have proved to be perennially timely), but the fact
of communal interpretation as our on-going access to God's transformative
presence. In this situation, trustworthiness is not in the timeless law but in the
timely, consistent and immediate justice and mercy of God that haunt the in-
nards of concrete historical events. It is my judgment that when Jesus is al-
lowed to speak from the world in which he lived, it is a Jewish interpreter we
hear. One critical dimension of fidelity to Jesus is a commitment to continuing

reinterpretation of the meaning of God in new historical, social and cultural situations.

One of the most timely instances of the need for a reinterpretation of Jesus' interpretation of God is a recognition of the limits of ''Father'' as a metaphor for God, and in some instances of the destructiveness of that metaphor. The limit of the metaphor is that it does not name that in our experience of God, the metaphor of mother or woman also interprets the character of ultimate reality. The destructiveness of the metaphor is that it easily supports patriarchy, a fundamental denial of the equality of women and men. The continuing exclusion of women from power structures in some traditions is a religious example. The lower wages paid women for performing the same work as men is a secular example, but one that is often pitched under the ''sacred canopy'' of religious reasons.

We are far from having decided how the next reinterpretation of God shall go. Will Goddess the Mother become a metaphor alongside God the Father? Will the Parenthood of God replace the Fatherhood of God? This will not be decided for a while because culture itself is grappling with the same issue. What is at stake is nothing less than some fundamental social reconstruction of the meaning of gender, and even the meaning of the human person.

Theologians and biblical scholars have long said that the Fatherhood of God is at the center of the message of Jesus. A commitment to reinterpret even that very center may be the moral obligation of fidelity to Jesus. Here again we confront the nature of interpretation: it not only seeks the meaning behind the texts, but more primordially projects new possibilities out in front of our lives. The project we call life is a different projection out in front of us when feminine as well as masculine metaphors about ultimate meaning collude with us to disclose new ways in which our stories as women and men might be told. This task is but one of the issues that confront us when we listen to the voice of Jesus as genetically related to the Pharisaic tradition.

Jesus as a person deeply formed in the Pharisaic tradition and therefore engaged in reinterpreting God anew based upon his own experience has not been addressed in our tradition. We have not taken that road. However, the recovery of this voice of Jesus seems to me to invite a quite fundamental reappraisal of the controlling influence of the Father metaphor. The feminist critique brings formerly excluded experience and new social instincts to bear upon the hermeneutical task. The better Pharisaic inclinations that belong to us as Christians because they belong to Jesus are inclinations that open us seriously to revising one of our most cherished images of God.

Although *Abba* language for God is not as rare in Jesus' time as Joachim

Jeremias thought, it was probably a mouthful for Jesus to move from the more formal "Father" to the intimacy of "Abba," or "Papa" as a commonplace name for God. Just maybe it is time for a new mouthful so that Mama is included with Papa.

Jesus a Synagogue Jew

Let me summarize at this point. In Jesus' time there were four principal Jewish sects: the Pharisees, the Sadducees, the Zealots and the Essenes. Through his early connection with John the Baptist, Jesus may have had some contact with an Essene kind of life. It is uncertain whether John had some connection with the Essenes, though he did opt for a desert life apart. But Jesus did not remain with John. Jesus does not live an Essene kind of life.

Nor was Jesus a Zealot. Efforts to connect Jesus with the radical Zealots have not been successful. Jesus is also clearly set apart from the Sadducees by his belief in the resurrection of the body.

While it does not seem likely that Jesus was literally a Pharisee, his teaching and his style are clearly Pharisaic, for the reasons given above.

There are so many details about the Pharisees themselves and about Jesus' relationship to them that simply and permanently escape us. We cannot be absolutely clear exactly what issues unite Jesus and the Pharisees, and what issues divide them, though it seems clear that the agreement is stronger than the disagreement. The synagogue is a Pharisee-directed institution; and Jesus is a synagogue Jew with sufficient education to be recognized as "teacher" (education is a synagogue function). In a word, it seems very likely that Jesus' consciousness was nurtured from the dawn of his existence in the *Halakhah*. Therefore, I judge it impossible to hear the voice of Jesus on its own ground without acknowledging a large genetic connection between him and the Pharisees. The points of contact that I have most emphasized are: further development of the axial notion of the individual, the concomitant internalization of the Law of religious life, and the way the commitment to relentless interpretation facilitates both of these movements of the human spirit.

We must now consider some other types of Jews that elucidate the life of Jesus.

Jesus as Teacher in Christian Scriptures

That Jesus was a teacher, that just about everyone around Jesus related to him as a teacher, and that Jesus thought of himself as a teacher: the Gospels are uniformly and strongly of one voice on this piece of history. To be sure, there are some clear analogies between a teacher in Jesus' time and a teacher today. But the socio-cultural situation of Palestine in Jesus' time is unlike ours in so many ways that it will take some thick history to let the teaching voice of Jesus speak out of its own world. We will first survey the Gospel picture of Jesus as a teacher, and then visit the social situation in which the Jewish teacher functioned.

The verb "teach" is frequently used to describe Jesus' activity. Jesus teaches in the cities, the villages and the streets (Lk 13:22, 26). He teaches along the lakeside of the Sea of Galilee (Mk 2:13), and from a boat just off the shore (Lk 5:3). He teaches regularly in the synagogues of Galilee (Lk 4:15), and when the day of the week that he taught is mentioned it is always the sabbath. He teaches in the synagogue of Nazareth where he was raised (Mk 6:2) and in the synagogue of Capernaum, his adult home (Lk 4:31). These are all in Galilee. He also teaches in the south, across the Jordan from Judea (Mk 10:1–2), and most notably in the Temple itself in Jerusalem (Lk 19:47; Jn 7:14, 8:20). When Jesus is queried at his trial about his teaching, he reminds Caiaphas, the High Priest, that he has always taught very openly in the synagogues and in the Temple.

Not only is Jesus described as teaching, but he is regularly called "teacher." The Jewish words for teacher are "Rabbi" or "Rabboni." The Greek word that most often translates Rabbi in Mark and Matthew is the common word for teacher, *didaskolos*. Luke, however, uses another Greek word as well, *epistata*, a "knowing" or "knowledgeable" person. We miss the sense of teacher in the usual English rendition of these words as Master, which does not suggest teacher to a contemporary listener.

Sometimes the Aramaic words for teacher are retained, an all but certain indication of the originality of the tradition in Jesus' history. In Mark, the earliest Gospel, in the transfiguration account Peter addresses Jesus as "Rabbi" (which Matthew changes to *kyrios*, "Lord," and Luke changes to *epistata*, "knowledgeable one"). Peter calls Jesus Rabbi again in Mark 11:21. And in Matthew, Judas refers to Jesus as Rabbi when he bargains to hand Jesus over, and also calls him Rabbi as he delivers the traitorous kiss. In John's Gospel, Jesus is called Rabbi by two of the disciples of John the Baptist (Jn 1:38), and John the Baptist is even called teacher once (Jn 3:26). Nathaniel and Nicodemus the Pharisee both call Jesus *rabbi* in John's Gospel (Jn 1:49, 20). The somewhat tenderer expression *rabboni*, my teacher, is spoken to Jesus by Bartimaeus the blind man (Mk 10:52), and by Mary to Jesus after the resurrection (Jn 20:16).

The Greek word, *didaskolos*, clearly means teacher. What we cannot know for sure is what Hebrew or Aramaic words *didaskolos* translates. It is likely, of course, that *rabbi* and/or *rabboni* lie behind the Greek word. However, both Jewish and Christian scholars have advised us not to import a later meaning of *rabbi* into Jesus' time. Jewish scholar Joseph Klausner says that in Jesus' milieu *rabbi* was not a fixed title and was used in current speech as an unofficial indication of honor.[29] Thus it may or may not have specifically named a teacher of honor. Martin Hengel takes this position too, and adds that probably by the time John's Gospel is written, *rabbi* is a more official designation of a teacher (and soon it designates an ordained teacher).[30] In my judgment, based upon Jesus' typical behaviors, *didaskolos*/teacher is not an inaccurate interpretation of *rabbi* or *rabboni*, if those are the original words. ''Teacher'' doesn't say everything there is to say about Jesus, but neither does it falsify an identifiable pattern of behavior between Jesus and his followers.

Just about all the characters who appear in the Gospels are reported as calling Jesus ''teacher'': people generally (Mt 17:24); a voice from the crowd (Mt 19:16); Jesus' own disciples (Mk 4:38; Mk 13:1), and sometimes the disciples by name, e.g., James and John (Mk 10:35), Peter (Lk 5:5, 7:40, etc.). Important people call Jesus teacher: the rich young man (Mk 10:17), whom Luke calls a ruler (Lk 18:18); the family of the Head of the Synagogue (Mk 5:35); the Pharisees (Mk 4:14; Mt 19:11); the Sadducees (Mk 12:19; Mt 8:19); and even the spies of the Chief Priests and Scribes (Lk 20:21). And the culturally despicable as well address Jesus as teacher: lepers (Lk 17:13) and tax collectors (Lk 3:12). And, finally, Jesus is said to refer to himself as teacher: find a room for the paschal meal, and tell the owner that the teacher has need of it (Mk 14:14).

We cannot establish that any of these instances is a verbatim report. But the evidence is overwhelming that Jesus is known as a teacher in his time and place. He teaches more formally in the synagogues and Temple, and less formally in the towns and countryside. To know what kind of figure a Jewish teacher is, we must look at that marvelous institution of the Pharisees, the synagogue, the schools attached to it, the educational system, and the kinds of teachers that provide education.

Synagogue and Worship

The Hebrew word for synagogue is *bet ha-knesset,* a place of gathering or meeting. Our English word ''synagogue'' is simply a transliteration of the Greek word that translates *bet ha-knesset.* The synagogue is the center of Jewish life and worship in the time of Jesus, common throughout Palestine and throughout the diaspora. It was typical of Paul to head for the synagogue wherever in his missionary journeys he appeared.

The origins of the synagogue are obscure. They are a place where the people gather to learn Scripture. While Ezra cannot be considered the founder of the synagogal structure of worship, the inspiration for the synagogue probably dates to his time. As I indicated earlier, after the Jews return to Palestine from the Babylonian captivity (535–536 BCE), Ezra is instrumental in collecting the principal Scriptures for Jewish life and identity, the Torah/Pentateuch, and having them read to the people in assembly. The Talmud speaks of synagogues during the Babylonian captivity, but there is no proof of that nor does it seem likely.[31] The proclamation of the Torah is a central ritual in the formation of Jewish identity. The synagogue insures the regular reading of the Torah. No one knows when the structure of the synagogue is institutionalized. The earliest archaeological evidence of a synagogue dates to Egypt, ca. 250 BCE.[32] Thus the synagogue appears to predate the Pharisees, though clearly by the time of Jesus it is under the provenance of the Pharisees.

In the time of Jesus, the synagogue is probably frequented only on the sabbath and on feasts; the market days (Monday and Thursday) were probably added later.[33] The day of the week is not mentioned for all of Jesus' appearances in the synagogue, but whenever a day is mentioned, as I have noted, it is always the sabbath.

The chief administrative person is the Head of the Synagogue (Jairus, in the Gospel, is one such). His assistant, the Hazzan, in effect runs the synagogue and is a sort of Master of Ceremonies. In contrast with Temple liturgy which is priest-oriented, the synagogue is lay in its structure and orientation. Knowledge of the Law and not priesthood gives a person—a man—the right to read and/or comment upon the readings in the synagogue.

The reading of the Scripture is the centerpiece of the synagogue service. The Torah is read in its entirety through a cycle of readings. The cycle is interrupted only by the special readings selected for particular feast days. The Scriptures are on scrolls which are kept in a place of honor. By the time of Jesus, readings are taken from the prophets as well, after the Torah reading. Any adult male can be invited to read the Scriptures. They are read in Hebrew—again an indication of some level of general education (for males, at least)—and immediately translated into Aramaic, the daily language of the people. The Targum is the written Aramaic translation. These translations are not merely literal renditions, but rephrasings that help interpret the sense of the Hebrew texts. An ancient text (P. T. Megillah III, 74d) insists that "anyone who translates a verse literally is a traitor," for every translation is an interpretation.[34] Meanings, not words, must be rendered in the language of "translation." The sermon upon the texts follows the reading. While there are schools for younger people (younger males, that is), the synagogue is in effect a continuing school for adults.[35]

Synagogue prayer is connected with Scripture reading. Though the exact prayer form in the time of Jesus is not certain, there is good probability that the *Shemone Esre* (in some form) and the *Shema* were customary in the time of Jesus. Scholars seem generally agreed that the eighteen Benedictions or Blessings of the *Shemone Esre,* which are still part of Jewish prayer, pre-date Christian times, although how they evolved is not clear.[36] Each blessing in the *Shemone Esre* is a praise of God. The Blessings in their present form are ancient, though the wording may not be exactly what would have been prayed aloud in the time of Jesus. In the second Blessing, God is blessed because "you are reliable in that you bring the dead back to life." Belief in resurrection is always a clear indication that we are squarely within the Pharisaic tradition. The *Shema* is the profession of faith par excellence for both the ancient and contemporary Jew (from Dt 6:4): "Hear, O Israel! The Lord is our God, the Lord alone. Therefore, you shall love the Lord, your God, with all your heart, and with all your soul, and with all your strength." When Jesus is asked what is the greatest commandment, he responds with the *Shema,* as would any faithful synagogue Jew of the time.

Synagogue and Education

The synagogue quite regularly has a school connected with it. The Palestinian Talmud indicates that in pre-70 CE Jerusalem there are 480 synagogues, each of which has both a "house of reading" (*bet sefer*) and a "house of learning" (*bet talmud*).[37] The house of reading is for the study of the Torah, the written tradition, and the Prophets are read as well. The house of learning is for the study of the Oral Law of the Pharisaic tradition. The educational system is inspired and supported by the Pharisaic movement. In the first century CE the majority of Jewish boys receive a formal education in these schools.[38] The Palestinian Talmud says that Simeon ben Shetah, president of the Sanhedrin during the reign of Alexander Jannaeus and Salome (103–76 BCE), ordained that all Jewish children (i.e., males) should attend school.[39]

Most male children in Palestine in Jesus' time attend school, even those from poor families. A child begins in the *bet sefer* at about the age of five or six, and learns to read the Scriptures, the Written Law. At about age eleven students move to the *bet talmud* where they study the Mishnah, the Oral Law. This concludes the formal system of education. After this most students take up their profession. A few of the most gifted students go on to a very specialized education with the true master teachers.

Study is not so much "study of" something, in our typically cognitive sense, though it is that too, but it is far more an initiation into a world of meaning. Since the Covenant which Yahweh makes is the critical meaning-making event for Jews, the study of Torah, Written and Oral, is itself an act of worship. As Safrai observes, "the study of Torah was a holy duty, the fulfilment of which became a religious experience . . . [it] brought the student closer to God."[40] In a similar vein, Erwin Goodenough observes that "in Judaism it was but a half-step from study to worship."[41]

The language of schools would have been Aramaic. Children would have studied Hebrew. Would the study of the Greek language or of Greek philosophy have played a role in the schools? The Babylonian Talmud records that a man who mastered the whole Torah asked R. Ishmael whether he might study Greek wisdom. After citing Joshua 1:8: "You are to meditate therein (Torah) day and night," R. Ishmael says, "go and find a time when it is neither day nor night to study Greek wisdom." In other words, "Don't do it!"

During the reign of Hyrcanus (134–104 BCE), a *Baraitha* (a saying in the Oral Law) records, there was a decree placing a curse upon a man who teaches Greek to his son. The Mishnah records a similar prohibition during the reign of Quietus, 117 CE (Tosafoth Baba Kamma 82b). Yet the Tosefta gives permission to the House of R. Gamaliel to teach Greek to children because it is practical to know Greek to interact with the Roman government in Palestine (Sotah XV, 8). After a careful examination of these and other texts, Saul Lieberman concludes that while there appears to be a negative attitude toward the study of Greek wisdom and the Greek language, the ban seems directed at children in their most formative years, and not necessarily to all people all the time.[42] Of course, we must keep in mind that the texts just referred to come from a much later period even though they purport to tell about the times in which we are interested. S. Safrai's conclusion is that during the second Temple period, no child studied Greek in either the *bet sefer* or the *bet talmud*.[43]

If there is a Greek influence (as seems likely), it is not in terms of educational content. That remains deeply and radically Jewish. However, the master/disciple structure that characterizes higher Jewish learning in Palestine may indeed reflect the impact of Greek life. One need only think of Aristotle, the peripatetic, walking through town with his students. The analogy, however, is but a formal one.

The Life of a "Great" Jewish Teacher

There is evidence for a school of advanced study by 50 BCE, a *yeshiva* or *bet midrash*.[44] It is not certain how many young students would have attended the *bet midrash* for higher instruction. Here we encounter a kind of apprenticeship to a great master teacher. Martin Buber once said that a good teacher is not someone who teaches a subject well, but one who, in the course of teaching any subject, allows the student to know the world the way he or she experiences it. Good teachers guide students in their experience of reality. That kind of education presumes a prolonged and intimate contact between teacher and student. Safrai's description of this relationship in first century Palestinian Judaism deserves consideration at length:

> There was the requirement of 'attending the sages' which was mentioned by Hillel the Elder and which was repeated in different forms in every age [*T. B. Nazir* VII, 56b; *Aboth de R. Nathan,* Version A 12 (p. 55); 36 (p. 109)]. Learning by itself did not make a pupil, and he did not grasp the full significance of his teacher's learning in all its nuances except through prolonged intimacy with his teacher, through close association with his rich and profound mind. The disciples accompanied their sage as he went to teach, when he sat in the law court, when he was engaged in the performance of meritorious deeds such as helping the poor, redeeming slaves, collecting dowries for poor brides, burying the dead, etc.

> The pupil took his turn preparing the common meal and catering for the general needs of the group. He performed personal services for his teacher, observed his conduct and was his respectful, loving, humble companion [*T. Negaim* 8:2; *T. B. Pesahim* 36a]. Some laws could not be studied theoretically or merely discussed, but could only be learned by serving the teacher. The groups which consisted of a sage and his disciples had property in common, or a common fund from which food was bought. At times this applied when the sage moved from place to place accompanied by his disciples. In some instances these arrangements became permanent. We possess tannaitic regulations which deal with the relationship between the sage and the pupil. They see him as "the brothers who did not divide their estate" or as "a father and his son" [*T. B. Erubin* 73a].

> Many sages were not content to teach at their local school, but wandered from town to town to teach the law. Study was not confined to the school or the synagogue, but was also carried on in the vinyard, in the shade of a dove-cote, in fields, on paths under fig-trees and olives and in the market. It was not uncommon for a sage to conduct discourses and discussions with

" . . . the requirement of attending the sages."

> his pupils in the town-square or in the market place, with the townspeople
> gathering around them and listening, irrespective of whether they were able
> to understand all or only part of the discussion [*T. Berakoth* 4:16; *P. T. Ber-*
> *akoth* II, 5c]. . . .
>
> As early as the time of the "pairs", e.g., Hillel and Shammai, we read of
> appeals addressed to the people to accommodate these wandering sages: "Let
> your house be a meeting house for the sages" (*Aboth* I:4). The public were
> invited to attend such gatherings: "Sit amidst the dust of their feet"
> (ibid.). . . . The nucleus of the listeners consisted of the sage's close ad-
> herents, but many others came [*M. Aboth* I: 4 and its explanation in *Aboth*
> *I:9 de R. Nathan* A 6 and B 11 (pp.27ff.). Cf. also *M. Erubin* 3:5; *T. B.*
> *Sukkah* 28 a; *T. B. Erubin* 54*b*; *T. B. Betzah* 15b]. The sage, generally,
> accompanied by a few of his pupils, was received and housed by some mem-
> bers of the local community who looked after their needs during their stay.
>
> Like their teachers the disciples supported themselves by their work and
> studied in their free time, occasionally under serious pressure. Others left
> home for a place of learning, and studied under their teacher for a number
> of years, sometimes if they were still single, but if married with the per-
> mission of their wives. There are many instances of wives being praised for
> enabling their husbands to study. . . . They were called students (*talmidim*),
> even at an advanced age and when they were old.[45]

It is immediately clear to any Christian reader how much the above description
resembles the pattern and activities of Jesus and his disciples. The great teacher
has his disciples. They travel together. They have a common fund. They pre-
pare meals together. When they gather for a lesson in the town square or under
a fig tree, others who are not disciples also gather and listen. When they travel
they are housed in local communities. The followers are sometimes older men,
and sometimes married men.

This is typical for Jewish teachers in Jesus' time. We Christians have
often thought of the activity of Jesus as utterly unique. But what we find is that
this kind of teacher would have been familiar in Jesus' time. I do not want to
claim much more than that, for the evidence does not warrant it. What I am
saying is that the master/disciples relational structure is hanging around in Palestinian culture in the first century CE, and the conduct of Jesus and his followers resembles that pattern.

Jesus' Education: Some Conjecture

We do not know anything about the childhood of Jesus. It seems safe to
presume that he attended a *bet sefer* and *bet talmud* as a child and young man,

because most Jewish males would have. His style of interaction with the Pharisees is not intelligible without presuming education. Whether Jesus sat with a sage after that, or followed a master teacher, no one knows. Because his teaching seems sympathetic to the school of Hillel, it has been suggested that his own teaching was formed in this school of thought. But that is conjecture. We can simply say that the "teacher" type does add some intelligibility to the life of Jesus and his followers.

The Gospels make clear that Jesus is at home in the synagogue. In first century CE Palestinian Judaism, synagogues and schools are signal expressions and creators of a new kind of Jewish life. Some commentators have tried to say that the synagogue is a substitute for the Temple which fell into some disfavor with the politicization of the high priesthood. But as Yehezkel Kaufmann insists, "in reality it was a new, original creation. The core of the service was not sacrifice, but the soliloquy of the heart and the utterance of the lips."[46] Synagogue and school are not so much two separate institutions as two collaborative and interrelated formative agents of Jewish cultural and religious identity. Sadly, the Christian interpretation of the Pharisees under whom synagogue and school flourished has been profoundly hostile for so many centuries that Christians have overlooked the immense fertility of these times. As a consequence, we Christians have missed the Pharisaic impulse as an essential élan in the soul of Jesus' life and teaching.

If "teacher" is a Jewish type that elucidates the identity of Jesus, there is yet reason for not subscribing totally to the justified and easy connection between master teacher and Jesus' life: many of these "teacher" characteristics make an appearance in another type of Jew, the wandering charismatic. And that is our next concern.

The Wandering Charismatic

The wandering charismatic is not, to be sure, a familiar daily figure in early first century Palestine. Yet he would be a readily recognizable phenomenon. Many characteristics of the wandering charismatic figure belong to Jesus as well. The wandering charismatic, though he resembles the teacher in some ways, is a more spectacular figure: he is a healer, an exorciser, a wonder worker. I will follow Max Weber, Geza Vermès, and Gerd Theissen in exploring "wandering charismatic" as a context helpful for listening to the voice of Jesus on its own ground.

Weber notes that what is indicated by the word "charismatic" is the fact that the authority of this figure is not derived from his or her legitimate position in the power structure of an institution. It is based neither in law nor in tradi-

" . . . a healer . . . a wonder worker."

tion. The power comes from somewhere else. The charismatic's authority is usually attributed to the holy man's (the *hasid*'s) relationship to God. Unlike the teacher who teaches what others have said or written, the charismatic figure teaches with an assurance that comes out of his own experience of God. Vermès lists several characteristics of the wandering charismatic figures in Judaism. The *hasidim* are holy men (none of them are women) "whose supernatural powers were attributed to their immediate relation to God. They were venerated as a link between heaven and earth, independent of any institutional mediation."[47] The supernatural powers are primarily three: healings, exorcisms, and effectiveness in prayers of petition.

Vermès also notes that while the wandering charismatic figure is not confined to northern Palestine, "this religious trend is likely to have had Galilean roots."[48] The northern figure of Elijah may well lie behind these later wandering charismatics, especially the recollection of his power over natural events. Some traditions about the wandering charismatics will help us develop a thicker history, and feel more concretely the analogies between the figure of Jesus and that of the wandering charismatics, some of whom are roughly contemporary with Jesus. "It is very pertinent to a search for the real Jesus," Vermès writes, "to study these other men of God and the part they played in Palestinian religious life during the final period of the Second Temple era."[49] In other words, Jesus the Wandering Charismatic must be understood within the larger framework of charismatic Judaism of which he is an instance. Like the other types, wandering charismatic does not give total insight into Jesus; but it is a valid even though partial one.

Honi the Circle Drawer (Josephus calls him Onias the Righteous) lived in the first century before Jesus, a charismatic figure, reported upon in Jewish rabbinic materials as well as in the work of Josephus. Like many of the wandering charismatics, Honi has power over evil (esp. over serpents), and he is also a wonderworker. The people know that his prayers to God work miracles. He is asked to request rain in a time of drought. When the rain does not come immediately, Honi draws a circle on the ground and stands in it. He prays, but it only drizzles. He complains that he didn't ask for drizzle. Then comes a cloudburst. Honi complains again that this is a bit too much. A third time he asks God for a rain of grace, after which it rains gently and normally. Vermès notes that Honi seems indeed impertinent, but that even rabbinic critics compare a saint's relationship with God to that between a tiresome, spoiled child and a very patient parent.[50]

Josephus reports that since Onias [Honi] is so successful in his prayer for rain, Hyrcanus has his people ask Honi to put a curse on Aristobulus. He refuses to cause this kind of turmoil between people who should not treat each other that way. When he refuses, he is stoned to death by some of the Jews who interpret his refusal as political neutrality.[51] While there is some likelihood that Honi is a Galilean, it is clear that Hanina ben Dosa, a pre-70 CE figure, is Galilean. He lives in Arab, near Sepphoris and only a few miles from Nazareth. Hanina was a healer. He cures the son of the famous Rabbi Yohanan ben Zakkai by putting his head between his knees and praying. Hanina can also heal at a distance. The son of the famous teacher Gamaliel (Paul's teacher) is mortally ill. Two people are dispatched to Hanina in Galilee. He prays, and then tells the two people to return home, that the fever had left Gamaliel's son. When the two return home and report what has happened, they learn that the hour Hanina spoke to them was the hour the fever left the boy, "and he asked us for water to drink."[52] Of course, the analogy with Jesus is striking.

Hanina is said to have violated the *halakhah* by walking alone at night, and by owning goats which the Mishnah disallowed. Citing other such violations by *hasidim*, Vermès notes that Jesus seems quite at home in such company.[53] It is not as though these people systematically disregard their entire tradition. Each of them remained within the tradition, and challenged it from within, based upon their own personal religious experience. What we are witnessing is a social characteristic of all living societies: a dialectic between charismatic and traditional authority, normally a self-correcting dialectic. If we are looking for reasons for some degree of historical conflict between Jesus and the Pharisees, notwithstanding his genetic connection to them, we probably find it here, in the conflict between charismatic and institutional claims.

Like Vermès, Gerd Theissen, in his *Sociology of Early Palestinian Christianity*, gives the wandering charismatic typology a central place in his interpretation of Jesus. But he does so from sociological perspectives which help "thicken" the history under consideration. Theissen cites four characteristics of these wandering charismatics. First, as wanderers they are homeless. When a prospective disciple tells Jesus he will follow him anywhere, Jesus reminds him that foxes and birds have homes, but the Son of Man doesn't (Mt 8:20). His instruction to his band of followers stresses the same theme (Mt 10:5–13). Second, the disciples are without family. To follow Jesus you must "hate" father, mother, wife, children (Lk 14:26). "Hate" is not a good translation; we are probably dealing here with the same Hebrew meaning used in a divorce. "Hate" does not necessarily imply rancor, but the radical choice to move two lives in fundamentally separate directions. To "hate" family means, therefore, to make a radical choice of Jesus as new family. Third, the charismatics live without possessions. They depend upon the hospitality of people in the local communities they visit: "Provide yourselves with no gold or silver, not even with coppers for your purses, with no haversack for the journey. . . . Whatever town or village you go into, seek out someone worthy and stay there until you leave'' (Mt 10:9–11). Finally, these people are to live defenselessly: if someone strikes one cheek, turn the other (Mt 5:38ff); if you are not received, just leave (Mt 10:12–13).

Unlike Weber's typology which stresses the personal characteristics of the charismatic figure, Theissen recognizes the causal interaction between factors at work in Palestinian society and the Jesus movement. The wandering charismatics are a radical phenomenon which can occur "only under extreme and marginal conditions."[54] Foreign domination is an extreme experience for Jews for whom their own nation is a Covenantal promise, and there are several resistance responses to it. One response is evasive, such as the large number of Jews in diaspora, or the separatist Essenes who retreat into the wilderness. The Zealots take up the violent response of guerrilla warfare. Theissen holds that the Jews of the south were more conservative because they were more dependent upon the Temple. Thus the more radical responses came from the rural areas, especially in the north. As I indicated in the previous chapter, the history of Galilee certainly indicates the presence of some revolutionary fervor there. Not incidentally, then, for the social circumstances Theissen indicates, Galilee rather than Judea is the more likely terrain of the wandering charismatics. In his wandering charismatic style, then, the figure of Jesus is not a stranger within Jewish life in northern Palestine.

Jesus as Prophet

It seems very likely that Jesus thinks of himself as a prophet, and that others regard him as such. There is no chance of working through all the interpretive layers that present Jesus as a prophet to arrive at a very secure judgment about the exact sense in which Jesus historically perceived himself and/ or was perceived by others as a prophet. But the prophet, unlike the teacher or wandering charismatic, is not a familiar figure in Jesus' time. There is fairly clear evidence that both the Torah and the prophets are proclaimed, interpreted and preached in the synagogue in Jesus' time. First century Jews continue to study the prophets, but they do not expect a recurrence of the classical prophet among them.

The rabbinic tradition, probably also reflecting at this point the early first century, is that "when the last prophets, Haggai, Zechariah and Malachai, died, the Holy Spirit departed from Israel."[55] During the Second Temple period, classical prophecy is basically no longer a phenomenon in Judaism. Jesus as prophet, therefore, is a more surprising presence than Jesus as teacher or as a wandering charismatic healer and exorciser.

Although Judaism in Jesus' time is not expecting new classical prophets, there is a clear expectation and a hope that a final prophet, an eschatological prophet, will issue in the final age. The final age is sometimes thought of as the restoration of Israel and sometimes as the apocalyptic beginning of a new age, ushered in to the accompaniment of great cosmic signs, a new age that is largely discontinuous with history as known up to that time.

Heschel's Psychology/Theology of Prophet

The thicker history that we hope can give us a sense of Jesus as a prophetic type will not be an attempt to summarize the huge amount of literature on the topic, but a very select presentation. I shall begin with Abraham Heschel's understanding of the classical prophet. Then we must look at the typology of the eschatological prophet whose appearance will be preceded by the return of Elijah. We will then examine Martin Hengel's presentation of Jesus as a/the eschatological prophet. The demand of Jesus to let the dead bury the dead is so radical a Jewish behavior that only the drama of the impending final age makes sense of it. We will then look briefly at Ivan Havener's new research on the Q document and its sense of Jesus as a prophet. Q is an early New Testament resource that comes out of Galilee itself or nearby western Syria. Finally, we will look at E. P. Sanders' sense of the historical figure of Jesus as a final prophet whose destructive behavior in the Temple (not really a "cleansing") is a symbolic gesture of the destruction of the old as a prelude to the new.

Abraham Heschel's two volume study of the prophets is his attempt to present the prophets phenomenologically, that is, based entirely upon the lives and testimony of the prophets themselves. In Heschel's company, I will return to a theme from the previous chapter: there is a dramatic contrast between the immutability and perfection of God in classical theism and the pathos and holiness of God in the prophetic tradition. The pathos of God is God's passionate connectedness to human history, with his own fulfillment at risk in how people respond to him. At the heart of the prophecy, and *in* the heart of the prophet, is a stirring sympathy (sym-pathos) with God's pathos. Heschel insists rightly that a divine pathos for us human beings is simply not possible if God is god in a Greek mode, as the following text from Aristotle makes clear:

> One who is self sufficient can have no need of the service of others, nor of their affection, nor of social life, since he is capable of living alone. This is

especially true in the case of a god, since he is in need of nothing. God cannot have need of friends, nor will he have any. (Eudemian Ethics III 1224b)

"If God is a being of absolute self-sufficiency," says Heschel, "then the entire world outside Him can in no way be relevant to Him."[56] However, the Hebrew experience of God, and especially the prophetic experience, fiercely denies the irrelevance of creation to God. To be fair, the classical tradition of course has struggled to find a philosophical way to justify God's care for the world, and that way is *agape*—utterly selfless love. But the unilateral love called *agape* does not square with the vulnerable God of the prophets whose happiness is dependent upon the loving response of those whom he loves. The God whom the prophets experience

is moved and affected by what happens in the world. . . . Events and human actions arouse in Him joy or sorrow, pleasure or wrath. He reacts in an intimate and subjective manner, and thus determines the value of events. Quite obviously in the biblical view, man's deeds may move Him, affect Him, grieve Him or, on the other hand, gladden and please Him. . . . Pathos denotes, not an idea of goodness, but a living care; not an immutable example, but an ongoing challenge, a dynamic relation between God and man . . . no mere contemplative survey of the world, but a passionate summons.[57]

That's how God feels the world in the testimony of the prophetic experience. This experience of God is better defined by the prophets than in the earliest Hebrew experience, but in continuity with it.

Heschel interprets the prophetic experience as one of sympathy with the pathos of God. Sympathy, as Heschel means it, is difficult to get hold of in English because our meanings are too mild (e.g., "I am sympathetic to that position," or "I extend my sympathy to you"). In sympathy, my feeling directly and immediately feels your feelings. I don't have the same feelings as you because I am responding to the same object of feeling that you respond to. In sym-pathos I feel your pathos, that is, your feelings.[58] There is a "harmony of being" that is at the basis of sympathy,[59] a "communion with the divine in experience and suffering."[60] Heschel says that the pathos of God breaks out like a storm in the prophet's soul; he is convulsed by it.[61]

The pathos of God is a moral pathos through and through, whose primary characteristics are justice and mercy. This is the feeling structure of God, and is the basis for God's values, and evaluates history. If the prophets felt these feelings of God, it is no wonder that they "knew more about the secret obscenity of sheer unfairness, about the unnoticed malignancy of established patterns of indifference, than men whose knowledge depends solely on intelligence and observation."[62] Heschel notes that the biblical meaning of *ruach* is often pathos, the same word, of course, that means God's Spirit.[63] The prophet is often interpreted as a man of *Ruach*, and when the English translation says merely "Spirit," it misses the notion of sym-pathos: the *Ruach* of God is a communication given to and received by the *Ruach* of the prophet. If Jesus is a prophet, then his age must not be surprised to see the return of the *Ruach* of God. Jesus speaks of the *Ruach*'s active presence; and Christians have regularly made the efficacy of God's *Ruach* in Jesus central to his identity.

Neither God nor prophet is finished responding to human situations by way of pathos. Each historical situation has wounds that must be healed, ruptures that must be mended, poor who must be fed, successes that must be celebrated, achievements for which gratitude must be sung. Pathos is completed with ethos: the concrete behaviors that are required of our lives. Heschel marks the connection between the pathos of God and *Ruach*/spirit. The prophets frequently note the efficacy of *Ruach* in their vocation. But prophets also say regularly that the *Dabhar*/Word of God came to them and gave some particular instruction.

> For my part, this is my covenant with them, says Yahweh. My spirit with which I have endowed you, and my words that I have put in your mouth, will not leave your mouth or the mouths of your children, or the mouths of your children's children, says Yahweh, henceforth and forever. (Is 59:21)

In the *Ruach*/Spirit, which can be interpreted as the pathos of God, there originates the justice/mercy structure of value. And in the *Dabhar*/Word of God, which can be interpreted as the ethos of God, there issues the existential word of address to the particulars of our historical lives. It is part of Yahweh's Covenant that Spirit/Word prophecy will continue its presence. And indeed prophecy breaks out once again in Israel in John and Jesus.

If the voice of Jesus is to be heard on its own ground, and if "prophet" is part of his ground, then we must interpret God as the prophets understood God. For Christians to take seriously the pathos of God means abandoning the interpretation of God found on the most travelled road, and conversing with the God of the prophets (including Jesus) on the less travelled road. The pathos of God must be taken seriously. If the real vulnerability of God to the world is to be believed, then so is his mutability. Conversation on this less travelled road puts the belief system of most Christian faith communities at risk. Faith itself is not at risk, but all its contingent expressions are always at risk, including even these we fashion now, to the best of our ability, concerning God's incredible ability to absorb the world concretely into divine joy and divine pain. It is surely in continuity with the deepest and oldest forms of Christian faith to think of Jesus as feeling the world with the feelings of God.

Let us return now to our consideration of the prophet. The behavioral characteristics of John the Baptist are certainly those of a prophet. The classic prophetic interpretation is used of him: "The word of God came to John the son of Zechariah, in the desert" (Lk 3:2). John preaches the nearness of the Kingdom and the need for repentance. Equally, many of the behaviors of Jesus are those of a prophet. He interprets his non-acceptance in Nazareth as the fate of a prophet who is never received in his own country (Mk 6:4). Some people say that Jesus is a prophet in the classical mold, "like the ones we used to have" (Mk 6:15, 8:28). The chief priests and Pharisees don't arrest Jesus because they fear the people who think Jesus is a prophet (Mt 21:46). We can be nearly certain that John and Jesus were experienced in their own historical lives as prophets by at least some of the people who followed them. But there is a most important variation in the type "prophet": not *a* prophet, but *the* prophet, the one who introduces the final age. Let us return for a moment to the pathos/ ethos of God, and the eschatological prophet.

Final Prophet and Two Eschatological Scenarios

It is Israel's experience that God is not just up to occasional pathos and ethos, but that God intends for justice and mercy *finally* to prevail. And in that *finally* lies an eschatology—a sense of a *final* time when the Reign of God is assured. Not infrequently this promise is related to the restoration of Israel, and to the peace of Shalom that a restored Israel extends to all the nations of the world. In this eschatological version, the accent is on intra-historical fulfillment.

In Second Isaiah we see an example of an intra-historical final age:

> The spirit of the Lord Yahweh is on me
> for Yahweh has anointed me.
> He has sent me to bring the [good] news to the afflicted,
> to soothe the broken hearted,
> to proclaim liberty to captives,
> release to those in prison,
> to proclaim a year of favor from Yahweh. . . .

> They will rebuild the ancient ruins,
> they will raise what has long lain waste,
> they will restore the ancient ruins,
> all that has lain waste for ages past.
>
> (Is 61:1–2, 4)

Luke has Jesus proclaim this prophecy in the synagogue, and claim that in him it is being fulfilled. This is perhaps a Lukan theological interpretation of Jesus rather than the historical voice of Jesus.

At other times in Jewish experience, the accent is upon the discontinuity between this age and the final age rather than upon their intra-historical continuity. In that case, great apocalyptic signs reveal the approach of the final age. Its inception is marked by cosmic events in the heavens and great turmoil on the earth, after which the reign of God is assured.

In the prophet Daniel we meet such apocalyptic imagery, imagery familiar to Christians because it has been used to interpret Jesus:

> While I was watching,
> thrones were set in place
> and one most venerable took his seat.
> His robe was white as snow,
> the hair of his head as pure as wool . . .
> A thousand waited on him,
> ten thousand times ten thousand stood before him. . . .
> I was gazing into the visions of the night,
> *when I saw, coming on the clouds of heaven,*
> as it were a son of man. . . .
> On him was conferred rule,
> honour and kingship,
> and all peoples, nations and languages became his servant.
>
> (Dn 7:9–14, passim)

In Matthew 24, Jesus' description of the final times is full of apocalyptic imagery, including a borrowing from the Daniel passage above. Even though the Christian Scriptures never explicitly call Jesus the eschatological messianic prophet, it again seems behaviorally clear that, whether in the restoration mode or in the apocalyptic mode, Jesus' life is compelled from beginning to end by his sense that the final time is dawning. It has already made its initial appearance and the time of fulfillment is close at hand.

Recent research indicates that throughout the Second Temple period, apocalyptic is an important, though not mainstream, trend of thought in Palestinian Judaism.[64] This style, characterized by rich use of symbols and images, thrives in periods of painful crisis. In the century before and after Jesus, there is a flourishing of Jewish apocalyptic literature. Therefore, if we ask whether the assumptive world of Jesus had access to apocalyptic imagery, the answer is surely Yes—though that does not prove that he used it. But at least those who used it of him were having recourse to interpretive metaphors that lay clearly within Jesus' own world of images. In the study of the Q document to which I shall return, Ivan Havener says that in this very early document Jesus is clearly an eschatological figure, "but only mildly apocalyptic."[65] I think what can be granted is that Jesus, in his lifetime, lived as the end-time prophet, proclaiming the immediate proximity of the Kingdom of God, and the radical change of life that it demands in the present. We continue this discussion now by turning to Martin Hengel's christology of the charismatic prophet.

Hengel's Perspective

Martin Hengel makes the figure of charismatic prophet central to his christology, but he comes at the issue from the perspective of Jesus' following: Why do people follow Jesus in the first place? What do they hear from him to which they respond? While Hengel acknowledges some familiar "Rabbi" patterns, he finds them insufficient. Teachers do not recruit students; students come on their own to the teacher. But Jesus recruits. Privileged students who follow their teacher do make huge personal sacrifices. But what Jesus asks is more radical by far than what any Rabbi/teacher could ask. Hengel finds the following text crucial:

> One of the scribes then came up and said to him, "Master, I will follow you wherever you go." Jesus said, "Foxes have holes and birds of the air have nests, but the Son of Man has nowhere to lay his head." *Another man, one of the disciples, said to him, "Lord, let me go and bury my father first." But Jesus said, "Follow me and leave the dead to bury the dead."* (Mt 8:19–22)

These words of Jesus are recorded in the Q collection of sayings which Matthew and Luke both use in their Gospels. The Q source is one of the earliest christological traditions, and early though it is, it still bears some interpretive imprint from the remembering community that recorded it. Yet the radical call of Jesus to leave everything, to be prepared for something radically new that is afoot—this is indeed the historical voice of Jesus. Jesus insists on the immediate response of leaving everything and everyone, even if the leaving divides a family against itself. The reign of God is the ultimate value to which all else must yield. Not to return to finish plowing the fields in order to follow Jesus immediately—that would be dramatic. But in the context of Jewish care for the dead, not to bury the dead is absolutely unthinkable—only at a time violently tensed between the old and the new might this prospect be seriously entertained. This is exactly what Jesus asks.

Teachers do not ask for that kind of radical commitment. But Jesus does, precisely as a proclaimer of the Kingdom of God whose breaking into history is imminent. "In the light of this urgent proximity, there was no time to be lost and so he had to be followed without procrastination and to the abandonment of all human consideration and ties."[66] The old dispensation is ending! The new age is dawning! The Gospels not only consistently portray Jesus as announcing the imminence of the Kingdom, but as knowing it directly through his own experience of God as his Father. This too seems unquestionably the historical experience of Jesus. And with this we come to a divide between what Jesus knows because his sensibilities have been nurtured by the Pharisaic tradition, and what Jesus knows from his immediate experience of God.

I agree with Hengel that the radical discipleship Jesus required only makes sense in the light of his eschatological proclamation. But two of his positions need a gloss. Hengel says that Jesus stands outside any discoverable uniform teaching tradition of Judaism, and that he cannot be assigned a place within the development of Judaism contemporary to him.[67] Clearly, the precise teaching of Jesus does not merely duplicate any contemporary teaching in Judaism, but that may only be another way of saying that sociological types cannot account for the concrete particularity of any figure who belongs to a type. What I have been at pains to suggest in this chapter is that Jesus accords easily enough with many aspects of Pharisaism, with the figure of a teacher, with that of wandering charismatic, with that of the eschatological prophet, and that his eschatology and mild apocalypticism are so deeply Jewish that he would not have been idiosyncratic in his time, neither typologically nor in the eschatological character of his teaching. That he was a surprise, Yes; but that he was an utter exception, No. I am not undermining the uniqueness of Jesus, but stressing his neglected yet remarkable continuity with his Judaism. That must be accorded him if we are to hear his voice on its own grounds.

Second, Hengel says that Jesus directed his disciples' gaze toward the dawning Kingdom and not toward everyday behaviors.[68] However, much of the teaching of Jesus is in fact concerned about how we are to be with each other in the world, though he means of course in view of the dawning Kingdom. Clifford Geertz writes that it is this placing of proximate acts in an ultimate context that makes religion, frequently at least, socially so powerful. It alters, often radically, the whole landscape presented to common sense, alters it in such a way that the moods and motivations induced by religious practice seem themselves supremely practical, the only sensible ones to adopt given the way things 'really' are.[69]

Jesus' concern for the immediately imminent Kingdom of God is full of requirements for how we are to live in this very minute. Conversion! Metanoia! Transformation of every aspect of our relational existence together because God is our Father! I would not press an argument about whether Jesus is more concerned about the coming Kingdom or about present behaviors. The two concerns seem of a piece in the Gospels, for the reasons and with the power that Geertz described above.

The Perspective of Q

Before considering the important new work of E. P. Sanders, let us look at the reconstructed Q document. In the Gospels of Matthew and Luke there are two kinds of similar material. Both Gospels consistently assimilate the text of Mark's Gospel into their own accounts, and therefore they share Markan materials. There is another batch of material which Matthew and Luke share, that is not found in Mark, which consists of sayings of Jesus. Most contemporary New Testament scholarship accepts that Matthew and Luke both used a collection of the sayings of Jesus as a resource for their Gospel accounts. An immense amount of constructive scholarship has gone into the reconstruction of this collection, called Q, and into the identification of its origins. I shall be following Ivan Havener's recent re-examination of Q.

The Q tradition is a very early one, at least as early as Paul, and maybe earlier. Q arises very near to, if not actually within, the Galilean area that Jesus frequented (in northern Galilee or western Syria). Havener concludes that ''Q'' had its beginnings in the ministry of the historical Jesus, and was a completed document before 70˚ CE.[70] This does not mean that the original band of followers sat down and wrote down Jesus' sayings. Q is ''a body of material that grew and developed.''[71] I would judge, for example, that the Wisdom materials in Q are probably a developmental layer, and do not originate with Jesus.

The community out of which Q comes seems clearly to be Christian Jews who still followed Jewish law and all the Jewish customs. They are tantalized by a Gentile who responds to Jesus with firmer faith than some Jews. Yet they still understand that Jesus is primarily addressing his own Jewish community with God's word. Q finally shows an openness to Gentiles, but never in Paul's sense of an active mission to them.

Q is certainly not interpretation-free. My point is that the interpretive layers are thinner, and are more likely to be based upon an assumptive world not dissimilar to Jesus' world (though not identical with it). And that is why Q is relevant to the project this book undertakes: its nearness to Jesus' Galilean horizon of consciousness, which more and more clearly appears to me as the road not taken. Havener says that the content of Q is "*almost entirely different* from what we find in Paul, and its view of Christianity challenges us to rethink the very beginnings of Christianity itself."[72] I think that the recovery of the Jewishness of Jesus basically has the same effect, and that the Q story is part of the recovery. As a Christian I must rethink my own Jewish identity. A first feeling response, one that I certainly own, is that of loss: there is a certainty and clarity about the Christian belief system that nurtured my identity as a human being, and I am asked to put it at risk and take a road I never took before. The gain—and I continue to speak for myself, and not for the entire tradition— is that my faith is radically historicized, and like a good Jewish Christian I can embrace the world and God together. Instead of feeling like a transitory pilgrim through time, I can affirm the essential relation between "Being and Time" (to steal from Heidegger!).

These ventures in continuing reinterpretation should be no surprise, of course. I have been insisting that every interpretation is both a response to an experience, and a free construction woven upon the experience. The free construction reflects, among other things, the differences of horizon between interpreted and interpreter. And here we are, twentieth century Americans interpreting once again the meaning of Jesus of Nazareth. Though we always remain tied to the event we are interpreting, our free construction is an essential component. When we respond interpretively to God's active presence in history, our free construction (which is part of all interpretation) participates in and shapes the event of revelation. Of course, the revelatory character of the free construction is always circumscribed: it is circumscribed on the one side by God's free initiative and on the other side by the interpreter's world view and cultural presuppositions.

How does Q's interpretation of Jesus differ, then, from later New Testament presentations of Jesus? First, in all four Gospels, Jesus has become the one proclaimed. But in Q Jesus is always and only the proclaimer. He does not focus his followers upon himself, but insists that his followers, along with him, focus their lives radically upon God and the in-breaking Kingdom of God.

In Q there is no suggestion that Jesus is God; "there is no confusion of the identities of the two with one another."[73] Jesus is called "Lord" in Q, but not in the same way that God is called Lord—for "Lord" can also simply be a title of respect in direct address. As Havener indicates, it is difficult to be unambiguous about the use of "Lord," which may or may not have christological aspirations, depending upon whether it refers interpretively to the risen Jesus (the "risen Lord"); but in any event, "Lord" is not an attribution of divinity to Jesus. Significantly, in Q Jesus is never called Christ. Q presents Jesus as God's son. But we must remember that "son of God" is a literary expression in Jewish speech. Just as "son of a liar" means a terrible liar, one whose entire life seems framed by lies, so also son of God names one who is very close to God and plays an important role in God's work; one whose entire life seems framed by God. The sonship of Jesus is first presented in connection with the baptism of Jesus and the introduction of the Spirit. God's voice calls Jesus "son." The nature of Jesus' sonship and relation to the Spirit continues as the Spirit leads Jesus into the desert where the tempter addresses him as son of God. When Jesus returns from the desert, his behaviors are consistently those of the prophet. Q, however, never directly calls him a prophet. But like a prophet, Jesus is in combat with the powers of evil, and proclaims God's message. He speaks God's word, and it is his own relationship with God that gives him authority; the relationship is so close that Jesus' person is inseparable from the word he proclaims. What Q does, then, is make a connection between sonship and prophecy: "Jesus is God's inspired prophetic son . . . [he] preaches authoritatively as God's agent to humans."[74]

Havener finds this connection between prophet and sonship unique as an interpretation of Jesus, but an interpretation insufficiently attended to because it has been overshadowed by the son of man sayings in Q. What Q does reinforce, and is important to our project, is that for Jews who followed Jesus radically and without ceasing to be fully practicing Jews, the sense of Jesus as son of God and eschatological prophet could account for their faith experience of God, working among them directly through Jesus.

Sanders' Perspective

I want to conclude this chapter with reference to E. P. Sanders' sense of Jesus as the eschatological prophet. Like Hengel who gave much weight to a few verses ("leave the dead to bury the dead"), Sanders places immense weight upon an incident that tradition has often—and incorrectly according to Sanders—referred to as "the cleansing of the Temple." More correctly, Sanders feels, we are confronted with destructive behavior that is symbolic of the end of the present age. What Hengel and Sanders both underscore is the radical eschatology of Jesus.

In his *Jesus and Judaism*, Sanders, like Vermès and Theissen, makes the figure of eschatological prophet central to his interpretation of Jesus' life and meaning:

> Jesus saw himself as God's last messenger before the establishment of the kingdom. He looked for a new order, created by a mighty act of God. In the new order the twelve tribes would be reassembled, there would be a new temple, force of arms would not be needed, divorce would be neither necessary nor permitted, outcasts—even the wicked—would have a place, and Jesus and his disciples—the poor, meek and lowly—would have the leading role.[75]

Sanders proposes that the eschatology of Jesus' teaching is that of the restoration of Israel, and the salvation of the nations in conjunction with Israel's restoration. What Jesus said about the Temple and how he conducted himself within the Temple precincts are, for Sanders, a clear indication of a restoration eschatology. That teaching and conduct belong to the historical life of Jesus, and would have been easily understood by his contemporaries as follows.

The Temple in Jerusalem, conceived by King David and built by his progeny, is a symbol of God's promise to Israel. The First Temple is destroyed by Nebuchadnezzar, and the Jews are taken into captivity in Babylon in 586 BCE. In 538 Cyrus allows the Jews to return to Jerusalem, and gives them back the sacred objects that had been plundered. In the spring of 536 work on a new Temple is begun. The "Second Temple" period lasts from 536 BCE until its destruction in 70 CE by the Romans. However, some major enhancement was added by Herod the Great in the generation preceding the birth of Jesus. Herod was at pains to ingratiate himself with the Jews and undertook for the Temple one of the jobs he was best at, masterminding the construction of huge, magnificent edifices. Those who have visited the recently excavated Herodian Temple construction are often awestruck at the elaborate and extensive work undertaken. Many of the foundation stones are immense, and still puzzle the contemporary imagination as to how they were quarried, brought to Jerusalem, and engineered into place. They must have seemed indestructible to a first century observer.

> As Jesus was leaving the Temple, one of his disciples said to him, "Master, look at the size of those stones! Look at the size of those buildings!" And Jesus said to him, "You see these great buildings? Not a single stone will be left on another; everything will be pulled down." And while he was sitting on the Mount of Olives, facing the Temple, Peter, James, John and Andrew questioned him when they were by themselves, "Tell us, when is

this going to happen, and what sign will there be that it is all about to take place?'' (Mk 13:1–4)

And with that, Jesus begins the long eschatological discourse in Mark's Gospel: the end of the present age, the beginning of the final age. It seems clear, then, that the Gospel's four questioners come to understand Jesus' reference to the destruction of the Temple in connection with eschatological hope in Israel.

At Jesus' trial before the Sanhedrin, the charge is brought against him that he said he himself would destroy the Temple and that God would rebuild it (Mk 14:57–58). Jesus was tried, convicted and executed. The reason for the crime is inscribed on the cross. It simply says that Jesus claimed to be the King of the Jews. Jesus did not make that claim, but it was apparently a Roman interpretation of his life. Immediately after Mark notes the inscription on the cross above Jesus' head, his Gospel relates that passers-by jeer at him that he said he would destroy the Temple. These remarks about Jesus from his trial and then at his crucifixion certainly add to the probability that the material about Temple destruction belongs to the historical life of Jesus.

Third Isaiah speaks of the final days as the restoration of Israel, where Yahweh will send peace flowing like a river (Is 66:12). Yahweh will make a new heaven and a new earth (Is 66:22). Ezekiel further says that the lands, in this final age, will be given back to the twelve tribes of Israel as part of the restoration. It belongs to the Q tradition that Jesus tells Peter, ''when everything is made new again [restoration] and the Son of Man is seated on his throne of glory, you yourselves will sit on twelve thrones to judge [govern] the twelve tribes of Israel'' (Mt 19:28).

Tobit is more explicit about the rebuilding of the Temple. Since it is composed around 200 BCE, it cannot refer to the rebuilding of the Second Temple as a future event. The Jews will again be scattered and regathered. On his deathbed, Tobit says that ''all will return from captivity and rebuild Jerusalem in all her glory, and the house of God will be rebuilt within her . . . '' (Tb 14:5).

In Jewish apocalyptic literature, both before and after the time of Jesus, the Temple theme is likewise sounded. A number of these passages are cited by Sanders, e.g.: ''the Lord . . . brought a new house, greater and loftier than the first'' (1 Enoch 90:28 ff); ''There shall be built a royal Temple of the Great one in his glorious splendor, for all generations forever'' (1 Enoch 91:13); etc.[76] Thus Sanders concludes that talk about the destruction of the Temple and the building of a new one would have been readily understood by Jesus' contemporaries in terms of restoration eschatology.[77]

All four Gospels recount that Jesus entered the Temple and began driving out people buying and selling there; he overturned the tables of the money changers and the seats of those selling doves. This is often interpreted as the cleansing of the Temple so that it can become a house of prayer. But as Sanders points out, the central religious act in the Temple is sacrifice. This requires that animals be available for sacrifice, that someone sells and someone buys, and that given the number of diaspora Jews who come in pilgrimage to Jerusalem, money changers are necessary. Sanders believes the "cleansing" interpretation was later added by those who did not understand the original context for Jesus' action as a symbolic event in which he dramatically enacted Temple destruction as a prelude to the final reign of God:

> Thus we conclude that Jesus publicly predicted or threatened the destruction of the temple, that the statement was shaped by his expectation of the arrival of the eschaton, that he probably also expected a new temple to be given by God from heaven, and that he made a demonstration which prophetically symbolized the coming event.[78]

It is often enough the case that the scholars themselves do not come to the same conclusions. Havener recommends Q as particularly trustworthy because of its early composition and its geographical proximity to the events of Jesus' life. In Q Jesus is presented as only mildly apocalyptic. Hengel and Sanders place Jesus' apocalypticism in much bolder relief, and feel they do so based on solid historical evidence. The historicity of Jesus' sense of himself as the eschatological prophet seems to me highly likely, whether mildly or boldly I do not presume to say. But once the Greek interpretations of Jesus in the *logos* tradition took hold of the christological imagination, the figure of the eschatological prophet was found wanting and heterodox. This was the Ebionite heresy, and it prevailed in the same areas whence came the Q source.

The probable historicity of the dimension of eschatological prophet belonging to the life of Jesus seems to me to require that we take it up again. We would do so not as a substitute for any other christology nor hold it alone to be a sufficient interpretation of Jesus. But it deserves to be developed more fully than it has as one of the many christological interpretations that belong properly to the Christian Scriptures.

Reprise

In this chapter we have thought of Jesus the Jew in connection with other Jews: Pharisees, teachers, wandering charismatics, and the eschatological prophet. We have carried on some conversation with him in each of the roles. Our primary concern has been to locate him within his Jewishness, not to differentiate him from that Jewishness. Conversation with Jesus *on his own ground* asks this of us.

It comes as a surprise to Christian sensibilities to learn from history that Jesus is far more like than unlike the Pharisees. There are differences, but not such as to turn Jesus away from their *haveroth,* which is a rather tight table fellowship. Jesus' table fellowship, however, embraces not only the Pharisees, but the outcasts as well, and distinguishes him from the protocol of Pharisaic *haveroth*—yet not enough to exclude him from it. These two features of Jesus' life have high historical likelihood.

Jesus lives from both the Written and Oral Torah. His freedom to reinterpret is a gift from the Pharisaic genius—they are the grand reinterpreters. As a Christian, I imagine that *our* fidelity to Jesus, like *his* fidelity to his *halakhic* tradition, means being simultaneously faithful to our sacred texts (our Written Torah) *and* to relentlessly reinterpreting God's action in Jesus Christ and in our lives located within the Christ-event (our Oral Torah). History moves on and so must normative appropriation of God's action among us, even of that action mediated through the life, death and resurrection of Jesus.

Jesus acknowledges that the Pharisees sit on the chair of Moses, and says their teaching should be followed. But when a prescription from *Halakhah* interferes with responding to a pressing human need (hunger, illness, suffering), the human need takes precedence. Jesus remembers that when David and his men were hungry and the sacred bread was their only possible food, they ate it. This "correction" feels to me like something that comes from the deeper and finer Pharisaic intuitions themselves—for they are meant to enrich and sacralize life, not to burden it. All of this is not to say that Jesus was a Pharisee, for I am convinced that he was not. We do, however, understand him more easily if we presuppose a genetic relationship between his consciousness and theirs, rather than the opposition and hostility that the Gospels, especially Matthew and John, indicate.

Jesus is also like another kind of Jew in his time, a teacher. The behaviors of both Jesus and his disciples suggest that he probably understands himself to be a teacher, and is related to as a teacher. While *rabbi* does not have all of the teacher-meanings it will later acquire, it does not exclude that meaning either. Already in Jesus' time *rabbi* seems to be emerging as a teacher title. It is the behavioral patterns, along with the many times that Jesus is called teacher (the Greek *didaskalos* means teacher and has none of the ambiguity of *rabbi*), that convince us that the title "teacher" belongs to the historical life of Jesus.

Exorcisms, healing, and working wonders of nature belong not to the teacher but to the wandering charismatic. And as Vermès and Theissen have demonstrated, Jesus, Honi the Circle Drawer and Hanina ben Dosa have accumulated very similar lore about them. This configuration of Jesus is strange to our imagination, but would have been familiar to the contemporaries of Jesus. The wandering charismatic is not a daily occurrence in all the small Galilean villages, of course. But Jesus is not an isolated example. The wandering charismatic is a religious "type" in first century Judaism.

Abraham Heschel describes the prophet as one whose own essential passions feel the world with the feelings of God. The prophet has sym-pathos with God's pathos. The prophet speaks with his own voice, but directly out of his experience of the world with God's feelings, and God has called the prophet to this. The gift of *Ruach*/Spirit and *Dabhar*/Word from God forms the prophet's identity. The Christian Scriptures give ample evidence that for very early communities the figure of the prophet illuminates the historical reality of Jesus, and probably even does so for Jesus himself.

Where Jesus parts company with the classical prophets is that while they often proclaim the coming reign of God, Jesus' proclamation marks the in-breaking of the Kingdom. He is rather the final prophet whom the classical prophets foresaw. Not *a* prophet but *the* prophet! Here too I am not asserting an ideological claim, but agreeing with Q, with Hengel and with Sanders, that there is solid reason for believing that the historical Jesus conducts himself as one who both announces and ushers in the final time, the Reign of God, and he demands an absolutely immediate and radical response. Before the final age could occur, there was the belief that Elijah must return to earth (Mal 3:23). Jesus says that John the Baptist was Elijah returned (Mt 11:14).

Christians easily read "Christ" almost as Jesus' last name, and usually through a Johannine filter (Christ as the incarnate pre-existent) or through later trinitarian Christology (Christ as Second Person of the Trinity). But it also has a differently loaded Jewish meaning. For literally, "christ" is an adjective that means "anointed." In Luke's Gospel, Peter says to Jesus, "You are the Christ of God" (Lk 9:20). When David does not kill Saul who has tried to murder him, David gives Saul the reason he doesn't: "You are the Christ of God" (1 Sam 24:11). No matter what, he could not kill God's anointed. It is in this sense, that the final prophet is anointed by God's Spirit, that Jesus can also be called the Christ of God. Of all the kinds of Jews we have tried to understand—Pharisee, teacher, wandering charismatic, eschatological prophet—the most fertile for christological conversation on the less travelled road is that of the anointed eschatological prophet.

But finally, as William James has said so simply and eloquently, "individuality outruns all classification."[79] Typologies illuminate individual character, but every individual human being is far richer and deeper and vaster than any and all typological abstractions. Why is it, James wonders, that "we insist on classifying everyone we meet under some general head."[80] All the types we have considered shed remarkable light upon the reality of Jesus. But alone or together they are inadequate: inadequate to Christians whose faith cannot be accounted for in types; and inadequate to everyone, lest the abstract be mistaken for the concrete.

I have not attempted to say everything true, only something true, and something true that does no violence to the essential Jewishness of Jesus of Nazareth. The retrieval of Jesus' Jewishness does no violence either to the possibility of Christian faith. But it is obvious that the quest for a non-supersessionist christological understanding of Jesus, which his utter Jewishness seems to require, does put many historical Christian interpretations at risk. All strong and real conversation puts its participants at risk, sometimes more and sometimes less. Conversation on this less travelled road is no exception.

Notes

1. Harvey Falk, *Jesus the Pharisee* (New York: Paulist, 1985).

2. Jacob Neusner, *From Politics to Piety* (Englewood Cliffs: Prentice-Hall, 1973), p. 50.

3. Solomon Schechter, *Aspects of Rabbinic Theology* (New York: Schocken, 1961 [orig. 1909]); superseded by George Foot Moore, *Judaism*, 3 vols. (Cambridge: Harvard Univ. [orig. 1927], 1962); superseded by Ephraim E. Urbach, *The Sages*, 2 vols. (Jerusalem: Magnes, 1979).

4. Jacob Neusner, *The Rabbinic Traditions about the Pharisees before 70*, 3 vols. (London: Brill, 1971); and a one volume condensed version, *The Pharisees: Rabbinic Perspectives* (Hoboken: KTAV, 1973).

5. Ellis Rivkin, *A Hidden Revolution: The Pharisees' Search for the Kingdom Within* (Nashville: Abingdon, 1978).

6. Neusner, PP 1973, p. 42.

7. Neusner, PP 1973, p. 50; Rivkin, 1978, p. 60.

8. Neusner, PP 1973, p. 54.

9. Jacob Neusner, *The Way of Torah* (Belmont: Wadsworth, 1979), p. 51.

10. Michael Cook, "Jesus and the Pharisees: The Problem as It Stands Today," *Journal of Ecumenical Studies*, 15/3 (1978), pp. 441–460.

11. Neusner, PP 1973, p. 51, citing Josephus.

12. Rivkin, 1978, pp. 211–251.

13. Elias Bickerman, *From Ezra to the Last of the Maccabees* (New York: Schocken, 1975), p. 67.

14. Karl Jaspers, *The Origin and Goal of History* (New Haven: Yale Univ., 1953).

15. Jaspers, 1953, pp. 2–5, passim.

16. Rivkin, 1978, p. 296.

17. Moore, I 1962, p. 114.

18. Moore, I 1962, p. 121.

19. Rivkin, 1978, p. 311.

20. Jacob Lauterbach, *Rabbinic Essays* (Cincinnati: Hebrew Union College, 1951), p. 92.

21. Rivkin, 1978, p. 297.

22. Cornel West, "The Historicist Turn in Philosophy of Religion," in Leroy Rouner, ed., *Knowing Religiously* (Notre Dame: Notre Dame Press, 1985), p. 46.

23. Cited in Rivkin, 1978, p. 260.

24. William Dean, "Hebrew Law and Postmodern Historicism," Presentation at Iliff School of Theology, 1987, p. 1., unpub. ms.

25. John T. Pawlikowski, *Christ in the Light of Christian-Jewish Dialogue* (New York: Paulist, A Stimulus Book, 1982), p. 89.

26. Dean, 1987, p. 13.

27. Dean, 1987, p. 7 (Dean's summary of von Rad).

28. Dean, 1987, p. 4.

29. Joseph Klausner, *Jesus of Nazareth* (New York: Menorah, 1979), p. 214, n. 16.

30. Martin Hengel, *The Charismatic Leader and His Followers* (New York: Crossroad, 1981), pp. 42–44.

31. S. Safrai and M. Stern, eds., *Compendium Rerum Iudaicarum ad Novum Testamentum: The Jewish People in the First Century*, vol. 2 (Philadelphia: Fortress, 1976), p. 910.

32. Safrai, 1976, p. 911.

33. Safrai, 1976, p. 918.

34. Safrai, 1976, p. 931.

35. Samuel Sandmel, *Judaism and Christian Beginnings* (New York: Oxford Univ., 1978), p. 147.

36. Sandmel, 1978, p. 148.

37. Safrai, 1976, p. 947.

38. Safrai, 1976, p. 946.

39. Safrai, 1976, p. 947.

40. Safrai, 1976, p. 945.

41. Cited in Sandmel, 1978, p. 147.

42. Saul Lieberman, *Hellenism in Jewish Palestine* (New York: KTAV, 1962), "The Alleged Ban on Greek Wisdom," pp. 100–114.

43. Safrai, 1976, p. 957.

44. Sandmel, 1978, pp. 142–143.

45. Safrai, 1976, pp. 964–966, passim.

46. Yehezkel Kaufman, "The Emergence of Judaism," in Leo Schwarz, ed., *Great Ages and Ideas of the Jewish People* (New York: Modern Library, 1956), p. 84.

47. Geza Vermès, *Jesus the Jew* (Philadelphia: Fortress, 1973), p. 79.

48. Vermès, 1973, p. 79.

49. Vermès, 1973, p. 69.

50. Vermès, 1973, p. 70.

51. Vermès, 1973, p. 71.

52. Vermès, 1973, pp. 75–76.

53. Vermès, 1973, pp. 80–81.

54. Gerd Theissen, *The Sociology of Early Palestinian Christianity* (Philadelphia: Fortress, 1977), p. 15.

55. Urbach, I 1979, p. 564.

56. Abraham Heschel, *The Prophets,* vol. 2 (New York: Harper & Row, 1975), p. 13.

57. Heschel, 1975, p. 5.

58. Heschel, 1975, p. 89.

59. Heschel, 1975, p. 88.

60. Heschel, 1975, p. 91.

61. Heschel, 1975, p. 88.

62. Abraham Heschel, *The Prophets,* vol. 1 (New York: Harper & Row, 1969), p. 9.

63. Heschel, 1975, p. 95.

64. For a summary of recent research, cf. P. Sacchi, "Jewish Apocalyptic," in the English edition of *Service International de Documentation Judeo-Chrétienne,* 18/3(1985), pp. 4–9.

65. Ivan Havener, *Q The Sayings of Jesus* (Wilmington: Glazier, 1987), p. 16.

66. Martin Hengel, *The Charismatic Leader and His Followers* (New York: Crossroad, 1981), p. 15.

67. Hengel, 1981, p. 49.

68. Hengel, 1981, p. 53.

69. Clifford Geertz, *The Interpretation of Cultures* (New York: Basic Books, 1973), p. 122.

70. Havener, 1987, p. 45.

71. Havener, 1987, p. 104.

72. Havener, 1987, p. 11, emphasis added.

73. Havener, 1987, p. 46.

74. Havener, 1987, p. 69.

75. E. P. Sanders, *Jesus and Judaism* (Philadelphia: Fortress, 1985), p. 319.

76. Sanders, 1985, pp. 81–86.

77. Sanders, 1985, p. 88.

78. Sanders, 1985, p. 75.

79. William James, RE 1967, p. 4.

80. William James, RE 1967, pp. 4–5.

WORKS CONSULTED
FOR VOLUME ONE

Abrahams, I., *Studies in Pharisaism and the Gospels* (New York: KTAV, 1967).

Altizer, Thomas J. J., et al., *De-Construction and Theology* (New York: Crossroad, 1982).

Berger, Peter, *The Heretical Imperative* (Garden City: Doubleday, 1979).

Berger, Peter, *A Rumor of Angels* (Garden City: Doubleday, 1970).

Berger, Peter, *The Sacred Canopy* (Garden City: Doubleday, 1969).

Bernstein, Richard, *Beyond Objectivism and Relativism* (Philadelphia: Univ. of Pennsylvania, 1983).

Bickerman, Elias, *From Ezra to the Last of the Maccabees* (New York: Schocken, 1962).

Biven, David, and Blizzard, Roy, *Understanding the Difficult Words of Jesus: New Insights from a Hebraic Perspective* (Austin: Center for Judaic-Christian Studies, 1984).

Boman, Thorlief, *Hebrew Thought Compared with Greek* (Philadelphia: Westminster, 1960).

Brown, Raymond E. and Meyer, John P., *Antioch and Rome* (New York: Paulist, 1983).

Brown, Raymond E., *The Church the Apostles Left Behind* (New York: Paulist, 1984).

Brown, Raymond E., *The Community of the Beloved Disciple* (New York: Paulist, 1979).

Buhlmann, Walbert, *The Coming of the Third Church* (Maryknoll: Orbis, 1977).

Burridge, Kenelm, *New Heaven New Earth: A Study of Millenarian Activities* (Oxford: Blackwell, 1980).

Chilton, Bruce D., *A Galilean Rabbi and His Bible* (Wilmington: Glazier, 1984).

Cobb, John B., Jr., *Beyond Dialogue* (Philadelphia: Westminster, 1982).

Cook, Michael, "Jesus and the Pharisees: The Problem as It Stands Today," *Journal of Ecumenical Studies*, 15/3(1978), pp. 441–460.

Cullmann, Oscar, *Jesus and the Revolutionaries* (New York: Harper & Row, 1970).

Davies, W. D., *Christian Origins and Judaism* (Philadelphia: Westminster, 1962).

Davies, W. D., *The Gospel and the Land* (Berkeley: Univ. of California, 1974).

Davies, W. D., *Paul and Rabbinic Judaism* (Philadelphia: Fortress, 1980).

Dean, William, *American Religious Empiricism* (Albany: SUNY, 1986).

Dean, William, "Hebrew Law and Post Modern Historicism," address given at Iliff School of Theology, unpubl. ms.

Endo, Shusaku, *Silence* (New York: Tappington, 1976).

Falk, Harvey, *Jesus the Pharisee* (New York: Paulist, 1985).

Fiorenza (Schüssler-), Elisabeth, *In Memory of Her* (New York: Crossroad, 1983).

Freyne, Sean, *Galilee from Alexander the Great to Hadrian 323 BCE to 135 CE* (Wilmington: Glazier, 1980).

Gadamer, Hans-Georg, *Truth and Method* (New York: Crossroad, 1975).

Geertz, Clifford, *The Interpretation of Cultures* (New York: Basic Books, 1973).

Goldberg, Michael, *Jews and Christians: Getting Our Stories Straight* (Nashville: Abingdon, 1985).

Goldberg, Michael, *Narrative Theology* (Nashville: Abingdon, 1982).

Goodman, Nelson, *The Ways of Worldmaking* (Indianapolis: Hackett, 1978).

Greenstein, Howard R., *Judaism—An Eternal Covenant* (Philadelphia: Fortress, 1983).

Handelman, Susan, *The Slayers of Moses: The Emergence of Rabbinic Interpretation in Modern Literary Theory* (Albany: SUNY, 1982).

Heidegger, Martin, *Being and Time* (London: SCM, 1962).

Hellwig, Monika, *The Role of the Theologian* (Kansas City: Sheed & Ward, 1987).

Hengel, Martin, *Between Jesus and Paul* (Philadelphia: Fortress, 1983).

Hengel, Martin, *The Charismatic Leader and His Followers* (New York: Crossroad, 1981).

Hengel, Martin, *Judaism and Hellenism*, 2 vols. (Philadelphia: Fortress, 1974).

Heschel, Abraham, *The Prophets*, 2 vols. (New York: Harper & Row, 1969, 1975).

Jagersma, H., *A History of Israel from Alexander the Great to Bar Kochba* (Philadelphia: Fortress, 1986).

James, William, *Essays in Radical Empiricism* and *A Pluralistic Universe* (Gloucester: Peter Smith, 1967).

James, William, *Pragmatism* (New York: Washington Square, 1963).

Jaspers, Karl, *The Origin and Goal of History* (New Haven: Yale Univ., 1959).

Kaufman, Yehezkel, "The Emergence of Judaism," in Leo Schwarz, ed., *Great Ages and Ideas of the Jewish People* (New York: Modern Library, 1956).

Klausner, Joseph, *Jesus of Nazareth: His Life, Times and Teaching* (New York: Menorah, 1925).

Kundera, Milan, *The Unbearable Lightness of Being* (New York: Harper & Row, 1984).

Lauterbach, Jacob, *Rabbinic Essays* (Cincinnati: Hebrew Union College, 1951).

Lee, Bernard and Cargas, Harry James, *Religious Experience and Process Theology* (New York: Paulist, 1976).

Lee, Bernard, "The Two Process Theologies," *Theological Studies,* 45 (1984).

Levy, Isaac, *The Synagogue: Its History and Function* (London: Valentine, Mitchell & Co., 1962).

Lieberman, Saul, *Hellenism and Jewish Palestine* (New York: Jewish Theol. Sem. of America, 1950).

Malina, Bruce J., *Christian Origins and Cultural Anthropology: Practical Models for Biblical Interpretation* (Atlanta, John Knox, 1986).

Malina, Bruce J., *The New Testament: Insights from Cultural Anthropology* (Atlanta: John Knox, 1981).

Marmorstein, A., *Studies in Jewish Theology* (London: Oxford Univ., 1950).

McFague, Sally, *Metaphorical Theology* (Philadelphia: Fortress, 1982).

McNamara, Martin, *Palestinian Judaism* (Wilmington: Glazier, 1983).

Meland, Bernard E., *Faith and Culture* (Carbondale: So. Illinois Univ., 1972).

Meland, Bernard E., *Fallible Forms and Symbols* (Philadelphia: Fortress, 1976).

Meland, Bernard E., *Higher Education and the Human Spirit* (Chicago: Univ. of Chicago, 1953).

Merkle, John, *The Genesis of Faith: The Depth Psychology of Abraham Joshua Heschel* (New York: Macmillan, 1985).

Meyers, Eric and Strange, James, *Archaeology: The Rabbis and Early Christianity* (Nashville: Abingdon, 1981).

Moore, George Foot, *Judaism,* 3 vols. (Cambridge: Harvard Univ., 1927, 1940).

Mussner, Franz, *Tractate on the Jews: The Significance of Judaism for Christian Faith* (Philadelphia: Fortress, 1984).

Neusner, Jacob, *Between Time and Eternity: The Essentials of Judaism* (Encino: Dickenson, 1975).

Neusner, Jacob, *Judaism: The Evidence of the Mishnah* (Chicago: Univ. of Chicago, 1981).

Neusner, Jacob, *The Pharisees: Rabbinic Perspectives* (Hoboken: KTAV, 1973).

Neusner, Jacob, *From Politics to Piety* (Englewood Cliffs: Prentice-Hall, 1973).

Neusner, Jacob, *The Rabbinic Traditions about the Pharisees before 70*, 3 vols. (London: Brill, 1971).

Neusner, Jacob, *The Way of Torah* (Belmont: Wadsworth, 1979).

Nicklesburg, George W. E., *Jewish Literature between the Bible and the Mishnah* (Philadelphia: Fortress, 1981).

Nolan, Albert, *Jesus before Christianity* (Maryknoll: Orbis, 1978).

Osiek, Carolyn, *What Are They Saying About the Social Setting of the New Testament?* (New York: Paulist, 1984).

Palmer, Richard E., *Hermeneutics* (Evanston: Northwestern Univ., 1969).

Pawlikowski, John T., *Christ in the Light of the Jewish-Christian Dialogue* (New York: A Stimulus Book, Paulist, 1982).

Peirce, Charles Sanders (Buchler, Justus, ed.), *Philosophical Writings of Peirce* (New York: Dover, 1965).

Rahner, Karl, "Towards a Fundamental Theological Interpretation of Vatican II," *Theological Studies*, 40 (1979), pp. 716–727.

Ricoeur, Paul, *Fallible Man* (New York: Fordham Univ., 1986).

Ricoeur, Paul (Thompson, John B., ed.), *Hermeneutics and the Human Sciences* (New York: Cambridge: 1983).

Ricoeur, Paul, *Interpretation Theory: Discourse and the Surplus of Meaning* (Fort Worth: Texas Christian Univ., 1976).

Ricoeur, Paul, *The Rule of Metaphor* (Toronto: Univ. of Toronto, 1979).

Ricoeur, Paul, *The Symbolism of Evil* (Boston: Beacon Press, 1969).

Rivkin, Ellis, *A Hidden Revolution: The Pharisees' Search for the Kingdom Within* (Nashville: Abingdon, 1978).

Rivkin, Ellis, *What Crucified Jesus?* (Nashville: Abingdon, 1984).

Robinson, James, *A New Quest of the Historical Jesus* (Naperville: A. R. Allison, 1959).

Rorty, Richard, *Philosophy and the Mirror of Nature* (Princeton: Princeton Univ., 1979).

Sacchi, P. "Jewish Apocalyptic," in the English edition of *Service International de Documentation Judeo-Chrétienne*, 18/3 (1985), pp. 4–9.

Safrai, S. and Stern, M., *The Jewish People in the First Century, Compendia Rerum Iudaicarum ad Novum Testamentum*, vol. 2 (Philadelphia: Fortress, 1976).

Sanders, E. P., *Jesus and Judaism* (Philadelphia: Fortress, 1985).

Sanders, E. P., *Paul and Palestinian Judaism* (London: SCM, 1977).

Sandmel, Samuel, *Judaism and Christian Beginnings* (New York: Oxford, 1978).

Sandmel, Samuel, *We Jews and Jesus* (New York: Oxford Univ., 1980).

Schechter, Solomon, *Aspects of Rabbinic Theology* (New York: Schocken, 1961).

Schoonenberg, Piet, "Trinity—The Consummated Covenant: Theses on the Doctrine of the Trinitarian God," *Sciences Religieuses/Studies in Religion,* Fall, 1975.

Schwarz, Leo, ed., *Great Ages and Ideas of the Jewish People* (New York: Modern Library, 1956).

Schweitzer, Albert, *Quest of the Historical Jesus* (New York: Macmillan, 1964).

Seltzer, Robert M., *Jewish People, Jewish Thought* (New York: Macmillan, 1980).

Simon, Marcel, *Jewish Sects at the Time of Jesus* (Philadelphia: Fortress, 1967).

Slonimsky, Henry, *Essays* (Cincinnati: Hebrew Union College, 1967).

Tcherikover, Victor, *Hellenistic Civilization and the Jews* (Philadelphia: Jewish Publication Society of America, 1959).

Theissen, Gerd, *The Shadow of the Galilean* (Philadelphia: Fortress, 1987).

Theissen, Gerd, *The Sociology of Early Palestinian Christianity* (Philadelphia: Fortress, 1977).

Thiselton, Anthony C., *The Two Horizons: New Testament Hermeneutics and Philosophical Description* (Grand Rapids: Wm. B. Eerdmans, 1980).

Thoma, Clemens, *A Christian Theology of Judaism* (New York: A Stimulus Book, Paulist, 1980).

Tracy, David, *The Analogical Imagination* (New York: Crossroad, 1981).

Tracy, David, *Blessed Rage for Order* (New York: Seabury, 1975).

Tracy, David, *Plurality and Ambiguity* (New York: Harper, 1987).

Tracy, David, Part 2 of Grant, Robert, with Tracy, David, *A Short History of the Intererpretation of the Bible* (Philadelphia: Fortress, 1984), chapters 16–18.

Umen, Samuel, *Pharisaism and Jesus* (New York: Philosophical Library, 1963).

Urbach, Ephraim, *The Sages: Their Concepts and Beliefs,* 2 vols. (Jerusalem: Magnes, 1979).

Van Buren, Paul M., *A Christian Theology of the People of Israel* (New York: Seabury, 1983).

Van Buren, Paul M., *Discovering the Way* (New York: Crossroad/Seabury, 1980).

Vermès, Geza, *The Dead Sea Scrolls: Qumran in Perspective* (Philadelphia: Fortress, 1977).

Vermès, Geza, *Jesus the Jew* (Philadelphia: Fortress, 1981).

Vermès, Geza, *Jesus and the World of Judaism* (Philadelphia: Fortress, 1983).

Watts, Alan, *The Book* (New York: Vintage, 1972).

West, Cornel, "The Historicist Turn in Philosophy of Religion," in Leroy Rouner, ed., *Knowing Religiously* (Notre Dame: Notre Dame Univ., 1985).

Whitehead, Alfred North, *Adventures of Ideas* (New York: Freepress, 1967).

Whitehead, Alfred North, *The Function of Reason* (Boston: Beacon, 1962).

Whitehead, Alfred North, *Modes of Thought* (New York: Capricorn, 1958).

Whitehead, Alfred North, *Process and Reality,* corrected ed. (New York: Freepress, 1978).

Wyschogrod, Michael, *The Body of Faith: Judaism as Corporeal Election* (New York: Seabury, 1983).

Index of Authors
and Subjects

About the Author

Bernard J. Lee, S.M., did graduate work in classical languages at The Catholic University, in theology and contemporary philosophy at the University of Fribourg. His doctoral studies were in philosophical and systematic theology at The Graduate Theological Union in Berkeley. He both taught and did research in Israel in 1982, and spent the 1984–85 academic year in research at the University of Judaism in Los Angeles. His teaching, lecturing and publications have encompassed ecclesiology, sacramental theology, christology, and the empirical tradition in process theology.

STIMULUS BOOKS are developed by Stimulus Foundation, a not-for-profit organization, and are published by Paulist Press. The Foundation wishes to further the publication of scholarly books on Jewish and Christian topics that are of importance to Judaism and Christianity.

Stimulus Foundation was established by an erstwhile refugee from Nazi Germany who intends to contribute with these publications to the improvement of communication between Jews and Christians.

Books for publication in this Series will be selected by a committee of the Foundation, and offers of manuscripts and works in progress should be addressed to:

Stimulus Foundation
785 West End Ave.
New York, N.Y. 10025